I0435702

Beyond the Inkblots:
Confusion to Harmony

by

Valerie Allen, Ed.D.

Revised Large Print Edition 2020

Beyond the Inkblots:
Confusion to Harmony
by
Valerie Allen, Ed.D.

Copyright 2012
Revised Large Print Edition 2020
All rights reserved

For more information, please contact:
Valerie Allen
VAllenWriter@gmail.com
ValerieAllenWriter.com
Amazon.com/author/valerieallen

ISBN-10: 1478146117 (Paperback)
ISBN-10: 1499194196 (Large Print)
ASIN: B008RNCCBM (ebook)
ASIN: B00HYO5X98 (Audio Book)

Dedication

This book is dedicated to all who have bravely shared their pain, sorrow, and disappointment. I have learned from those who have triumphed over difficulty, succeeded despite obstacles, and created the satisfying life they deserve. You have my sincere appreciation.

Deepest Appreciation

I am grateful to the readers and editors who shared their skills, talents, and support to make this book possible: Parker Allen, Valerie Gray, and Holly Fox Vellekoop. I appreciate the encouragement and support from the *Space Coast Writers' Guild*, *Authors for Authors*, and the *Cape Canaveral Branch of the National League of American Pen Women*.

Valerie Allen
Melbourne, Florida

Beyond the Inkblots:
Confusion to Harmony

by

Valerie Allen, Ed.D.

Contents

Great Explorations
Self Report
Life's Big Questions
Discovery
Empowerment

Life is a Do-It-Yourself Project

Wherever You Go, There You Are
Surprise, Surprise, Surprise
Living vs. Existing
Your Personal Happiness Meter
Up and Down You Go
Plan A vs. Plan B
Presto-Change-o!
        Plan B Becomes Plan A
Proactive vs. Reactive

Persecute, and then Rescue the Victim
It's Your Turn to Call
The Bounce Back Kid

A Wedding of Clones
Lose-Lose Situations
Fool Me Once, Shame on You,
      Fool Me Twice, Shame on Me
I Am, I Can, and I Will
The Undecided
Life Enriching Principles

Think Big, Move Fast
Life by Default
Imagine and Believe
Who Shot Me in the Foot?
Ready, Aim, Fire
Who's In Charge Here?
Why Give Up Before It's Over?
Is It Really the End of the World?
Success and Happiness

Bridge

There is a bridge

from your heart to mine

Reaching across, it pulls us together.

Stretching over unknown waters

It connects us in ways

we have yet to learn.

The bridge shows us

how much we are alike

Yet in so many ways,

different, as well.

Bringing us closer

There is a bridge.

Shannon Sullivan
Harrisburg, NC

~ *Introduction* ~

Great Explorations

This book is meant as a journey with musings about life's big questions. It is a place to begin a search and rescue mission for your true self. As you ponder where you are in life, how you got there, and where you want to be, there are no right or wrong answers. There is only understanding and insight.

This book presents an opportunity to assess your thoughts, feelings, and actions. This is not a place to pass judgment or criticize. This is a place of self-discovery, to leave confusion behind and find harmony in your life.

Self Report

There are times when we're not sure where we are. We wonder if we're losing ground as we journey through life. We assess ourselves mentally, physically, emotionally, and spiritually. We look at the status of our finances, career, and relationships. Is one area out of balance? Are we consumed in one area to the exclusion of others? Are we out of sync with ourselves?

When we are willing to look deeply into our inner self, gain understanding of our past, and proactively move forward, we will gain insight and be open to the challenge of a better life. We will create the life we want and deserve.

Life's Big Questions

Take a few minutes to ponder these questions. Allow your thoughts to go unchecked and make no judgments.

- *Where am I now?*

- *How did I get here?*

- *Is this where I want to be?*

- *What do I want?*

- *Where do I go from here?*

- *How do I get to where I want to be?*

- *How soon will I begin to move forward?*

Discovery

There is no need to fret about the answers to these questions. You are about to begin a journey of discovery. As you read this book, you will find answers, but also some new questions. You can sit back and assess, evaluate, and analyze your life in the privacy and comfort of your inner thoughts.

You can discover the good and loving person you are despite the upheavals you have experienced in life. You can take charge and be in control of whom you are and where you want to be. You can take yourself there.

Empowerment

To empower is to give yourself authority, to allow, to permit, to enable yourself to take charge of your life. Emotional pain forces us to look at where we are, wonder how we got there, ponder where we want to be, and make plans to change. When emotionally distressed and dissatisfied we begin to explore our feelings about life and relationships.

This book is written for those who want to enhance the quality of life, develop their potential, and find inner peace.

You can have a better, more fulfilling life. You may feel your needs are not being met and your goals haven't been reached. You may be filled with fear and self-doubt. You may feel time is running out. You may vacillate between quiet frustration to overflowing rage. Something has caused a feeling of disequilibrium; you are not comfortable within yourself. These stirrings urge you to move on in life, look deeper, quest for more, find satisfaction, grow, and change. You can move from confusion to harmony.

*~ **There is a purpose in all things** ~*

Chapter 1

Life is a Do-It-Yourself Project

Wherever You Go, There You Are

You cannot escape your life; you cannot exchange it for one you think you may like better. It might be nice if you could push the rewind button and edit a few things in your past, but you cannot change things that have already happened. You cannot "un-ring" the bell. It is critical to understand it is not what happens to you, it is how you handle what happens that determines the quality of your life. You bring yourself to every situation. This is where you are now. Suffice it to say, you are here, and wherever you go, there you are.

Surprise, Surprise, Surprise

The surprising thing about life is that we are here at all. There is a significant investment of time, money, and debate by scientists, theologians, physicians, and politicians to determine when human life begins and when it ends. Each of us holds a personal belief about the phenomenon we call a "living human being."

The proliferation of fertility clinics validates the struggle for conception. The journey from conception to birth is perilous at best, fraught with the possibilities of biological and medical mishaps. The survival of a newborn is totally dependent on the beneficence of others. Although, we may hold differing beliefs about when human life begins, we do know between our *birth* and our *death*, we are here, among the living, and so our journey begins.

Living vs Existing

There is, however, a difference between living and existing. We all know people who are old at 40 and those who are young at 70.

What a pleasure it is to be around those positive individuals who exude hope and enthusiasm. These people seek opportunities for happiness, radiate well-being, and impress us with their confidence. They arise each day with the expectation of success and happiness. They embrace change. They find goodness in their everyday lives. These people are truly living.

Some people only exist. They seem to be marking time, tolerating their day-to-day existence. They age with little joy, happiness, or hope for the future. They bemoan their past, complain about their empty lives, and see nothing pleasant in their future. They are miserable and unpleasant to be around. These people are existing not living.

Your Personal Happiness Meter

You may feel tired, worn out, and hopeless. Some days it may be a struggle to get up in the morning. You drag through the day and do the minimum to get by, without pleasure, without expectations. You may have sleep problems or eating problems; you may have headaches or back aches; you may have strange, elusive pains. You may feel out of sorts and at odds with yourself and the world, lonely, and isolated. You may have an awful feeling that your life is out of control. You feel overwhelmed and helpless to make things better.

Life is a struggle and you feel weary. You have given up hope; your world is falling apart. Every problem becomes a crisis and trivial things cause exaggerated responses. You feel lost and alone, and no one seems to care. You may have learned how to *exist* without *living*.

How did you arrive at this awful state of being? Some of us are able to pinpoint the exact event that triggered the physical and emotional turmoil we are suffering. Others simply can't remember life any other way.

You may think about your childhood, your family, your spouse, your ex-spouse, friends, and significant others. You talk about love and marriage, bitterness and breakups, heartbreak and rejection. You weep about children and step-children, the disappointment of having no children, and the pain of losing a child. You talk about a great job and no job, financial security, and abject poverty. You harbor family secrets.

You recall living with Mom, Dad, or Grandma. You experience growing up in foster homes or on the streets. You feel the rejection of parents, siblings, friends, teachers, or co-workers. You hurt from being used and abused by others. You suffer cruel betrayal. You re-experience the pain and the fear of medical problems, your own and others. You know about rejection: feeling unloved and unwanted.

Yet somehow, you survived. Through all this turmoil, you found relief. You began to "feel" again. Fears subsided, you felt secure, and found peace. You experienced renewal, no longer just drifting from one day to the next. You enjoy the quality of life, which has been denied, or missing for so long. Slowly you integrated your past with the present and began to look to the future with hope. You came back to life!

What miracle brings about such change? What phenomenon takes place? Our past has not been reconstructed and there hasn't been a drastic change in our current circumstances. Instead, you took charge of your life with a new found ability to change, adapt, and perceive differently. You set a goal, made a plan, and took action. You empowered yourself to create the life you wanted to find happiness and enjoy inner peace.

Up and Down You Go

There are no good or bad emotions. Our emotions are simply responses we experience when faced with various situations. Problems arise when you allow yourself to become emotionally overwhelmed. You may then engage in maladaptive behavior to the point you cannot function effectively in your day-to-day life.

At times life seems like a gigantic, emotional roller coaster, moving fast and in unexpected ways. However, emotions prompt you to think, feel, and take action. To maintain emotional balance you must:

- Pinpoint how you feel: anger or rage, loved or tolerated, hurt or humiliated, and so on.

- Know the exact trigger for your emotions: a person, a task, or a situation

- Respond in an effective, appropriate, and socially acceptable manner.

Let's look at an example. If you are miserable each day at the thought of going to work, you need to listen to yourself. What is your exact emotional response? Are you angry, frustrated, or afraid? What part of "work" is making you feel bad or ill at ease?

Break down each step of "work" and explore which ones you find problematic. Stay in touch with your emotions as you think about each of these steps:

- Getting up early; coming home late

- Driving a long distance; driving through heavy traffic
- Unfriendly coworkers; critical management; ineffective administration
- Mandatory dress code; uniforms
- Unpleasant or unsafe work environment; inadequate parking
- Specific job skills; task performance requirements
- Meeting deadlines; unreasonable demands
- Boring work; no incentive for high quality job performance
- No career growth; no hope of advancement

Identify which step was your emotional trigger. Instead of

generalizing such beliefs as, "I hate going to work," or "I can't stand my job," specify what aspect of your employment upsets you the most. After identifying your emotional response to each step, you will be able to focus on the exact source of your discomfort about work. Now you can focus on and work to resolve the specific problem without generalizing excessive emotional distress toward your job.

Plan A vs. Plan B

We all hope for *Plan A*, nevertheless, often wind up dealing with *Plan B*—the unexpected. In life, we aim for the highest achievement, plan on success, and expect the best. *Plan B* is not a substitute for *Plan A*, it is a temporary detour. *Plan B* may be a set back, but you can deal with it and by so doing, eliminate a stumbling block on the road to *Plan A*.

Happy, successful people develop a firm belief in their resiliency and self-efficacy. To believe You will never face adversity, that nothing bad will ever happen or misfortune will never come your way is unrealistic. These beliefs set you up for frustration and disappointment.

Instead, you must come to know and believe when faced with a challenge, you will rise to the occasion with your best and fullest resources. Our goal is not to wish and hope an adverse event will not happen. Our goal is to prepare and take action that will resolve or improve the situation if and when it does occur. You need to adapt to *Plan B* to bring about the least harmful result, the least hurt, and ultimately, the best outcome, given the situation.

Of course, sometimes strange things happen to *Plan A* along the way. Often, when forced to deal with *Plan B*, you learn, you grow, and you change. Sometimes we replace our *Plan A* with our *Plan B*. This can happen because we realize we enjoy and are better suited to *Plan B* than we were to *Plan A*. A switch from *Plan A* to *Plan B* could be a matter of economic necessity, family crises, or a change in opportunities. It is not always a bad thing to replace *Plan A* with *Plan B*.

Presto-Change-o!
Plan "B" becomes Plan "A"

Here is one of my personal experiences. In the course of one afternoon, my *Plan B* became my *Plan A*. One of my first jobs after high school was working in a medical office. I was fascinated with the diagnostic skill of the physician. He listened attentively and had a keen sense of observation. He was a true healer with a blend of caring and skill.

I was so inspired by this man I decided I too would become a physician. This became my *Plan A*. To this end, I enrolled in the College of Science at a university. I worked my way through college employed in a hospital, medical offices, and clinics. I applied for loans and grants to finance my four-year degree and applied to medical schools for graduate studies.

Along the way, I fell in love, married, and had children. I endured long hours of study, travel to and from the university, and the day-to-day issues of caring for my family. Sleep became a luxury I longed for, and personal time was nonexistent. I made few complaints. I knew the path I had chosen, and was fueled by one day fulfilling my dream. I was fully committed to my *Plan A*, to become a physician. Then it happened—along came *Plan B*.

During my third year of pre-med, in the midst of obtaining more loans, and making application to medical schools, a family member became seriously ill and was diagnosed with a chronic, incurable medical condition. My life became one of even more limited financial resources, high medical expenses, and a shift in family responsibilities. My *Plan B* included the decision to give up *Plan A*: my dream of becoming a physician. Reality was a lack of funds and time to finish the rigorous course of study needed to complete my medical degree.

Plan B quickly became my focus; *Plan B* was my new *Plan A*. I sought counsel with the university staff to salvage my three years of college and ward off demands of premature student loan payments. With only one year of funds remaining, what degree could I complete and apply all the credits I had earned thus far? There was only one program available, Elementary Education Teacher.

In one afternoon, I went from *Plan A*: being a physician to *Plan B*: being an elementary school teacher. I left the College of Science and applied to the College of Education. After a review of the requirements to complete the necessary course work and obtain my teaching certificate, I realized I could do this in the one year of funds remaining.

I had never explored the possibility of a career in education. Other than my own schooling, I had no clue what it entailed. Nevertheless, faced with the loss of *Plan A* and the reality of *Plan B*, I threw myself into the curriculum demands and requirements to become a certified teacher. My new plan was to finish my degree within the year and obtain full time gainful employment. This was now my *Plan A*.

Was I settling for second best? Was I talking myself into seeing the up side of this situation? To some extent, this was true. It was not easy to give up *Plan A*; especially realizing this was a final decision in my life. This was not a temporary set back; this required an entire new direction. Was I willing to put the needs of my family first and give up my career ambition?

When you are faced with events and life decisions, you make choices. It is your responses that lead you to choose one path and not another. This is how you develop your personal and unique life.

Over the course of time, my career moved from medicine to education to mental health. My *Plan A*, to become a physician, was replaced by *Plan B,* to become an educator. This was based on a situation beyond my control; however, I alone had to make the decision between caring for my family and a new career direction. Thus, my *Plan B* replaced my *Plan A.* Years later, my revised *Plan A,* to become an educator, evolved into yet a different *Plan A,* to enter the field of mental health.

We all start with *Plan A* in mind. Over time, due to circumstances, we make choices. Our decisions take us in new directions, with different possibilities. How we deal with these challenges makes all the difference. Do we choose the comfort and safety of what we know or do we choose the road less traveled? It's not the events, but our decision in how to handle them that brings us to where we are in life.

Proactive vs Reactive

You did not have total control of how you got to where you are, but you have the ability to set your own goals and determine the road you will take. You can decide to give up at each hurdle, or work your way around it and keep going. You need to take charge of your life. Anticipate reality: things will go wrong, you may change your mind, and there will be delays in reaching your goals. This does not mean failure, it means an opportunity to grow and change.

You determine your life's agenda, based on your needs and values. You must understand yourself and know what you expect of others. Your decisions should be based on your emotional strength and self-confidence. You need to be proactive in identifying and meeting your own needs, not reactive to the behavior or needs of others.

When you find yourself in the *If only* or the *Wait until* life style, you are putting off living based on some external event, over which you may have little or no control. Consider the "What if" life style. *What if I don't live that long? What if I wait until it's too late?* As you debate how to act or react, life moves on. It is better to make a decision, than to be lost to indecision.

~ *Get yourself together* ~

Chapter 2

The Three Faces of You

It's All About Me

How did we become who we are? There are three basic factors that create the person we have turned into: genetics, environment, and personality. The intricate blend of these three factors creates each unique individual. With millions of people in this world, no two are exactly alike. Even identical twins, with the same genetic make up, raised in the same environment, are not the same person.

DNA: A Mutual Donation

Genetics are based on our deoxyribonucleic acid, more commonly called DNA. This is the biochemical building blocks of our cellular and physical selves. It contains the genetic instructions used in the development and function of all living organisms. Sections of DNA that carry genetic material are called genes. Within each cell, DNA is organized into chromosomes. When a cell divides, our chromosomes are duplicated and the DNA is replicated in each new cell.

This complex set of proteins, mixed and matched over time, is unique within each of us. Our DNA comes directly from our biological parents, however, there were generations of family members on both sides who contributed as well to our DNA. When we're told we have Grandma's eyes, or Great Granddad's build this reflects the DNA passed on to us by our ancestors.

DNA relates to fixed attributes such as our eye and skin color. There are also medical conditions directly related to genes laid down through DNA. It is important to understand

DNA does not give us *bad behavior genes*, *unhappy genes*, and so on. We are not born bad or good, happy or unhappy based on our DNA. We have learned behaviors, which affect our actions and reactions in given situations.

DNA is a fixed part of us, although scientists are tinkering with it. Methods have been developed to purify DNA and manipulate it. These techniques of man-made DNA are known as recombinant technology. DNA has been modified, changed, and used to create clones.

The positive benefits of recombinant DNA could be longer life, improved health, or elimination of genetic disorders. The negative outcome could be human engineering to create superior and inferior life forms. The influence of politics and money has created ethical and moral issues surrounding man-made DNA.

We Can Choose Our Friends; We Are Blessed With Our Relatives

In addition to our DNA, a major influence on who we are and who we become is our environment. This is the question of *Nature* vs *Nurture*. Nature is our given DNA, our specific genetic make up. Nurture is the environment in which we live.

This complex set of factors and experiences have a major impact on the direction of our lives. However, if environment were the sole dictator of our behavior, it is unlikely a teacher's child would drop out of school, a police officer's child would shoplift, or a minister's child would tell a lie. Conversely, the child of an alcoholic would drink, the child of a criminal would commit crimes, and the child of a drug user would be an addict. Although these things sometimes happen, reality suggests this line of reasoning is far from absolute.

Our environment begins at the moment of conception, which is different for each of us. Consider a child born to a young, healthy married couple or the infant born to a malnourished, unmarried, homeless, 15-year-old girl.

The fetus floats within the mother's womb absorbing whatever nutriments are available. The unborn child responds to prenatal vitamins or illegal drugs. He or she is exposed to the mother's health and living conditions, whether in a supportive household or a juvenile treatment center. The unborn child has no control over these preexisting environmental factors, yet these conditions have a serious impact on his or her survival during fetal development and after birth.

We all enter this world without choice of family or circumstances. Later in life, we can choose with whom we associate, but we cannot choose our ancestors. There is a vast difference in the environmental factors affecting each of us.

As an infant, you were not born angry, anxious, or depressed. You were not intent on criminal acts or mischievous behavior. You were innocent. You were born into this world with a specific genetic and biological make up. You were also born into a certain life style and family circumstance. As a child, you were pushed and pulled, bent and molded, to fit in and adapt to your environment.

An infant born into a loving, nurturing family, willing and able to provide beyond the basics of food, clothing, and shelter starts life with positive advantages. This baby will have the benefits of extended family, educational opportunities, and social enrichment. The family supports the youngster in community activities, such as the church choir, school, sports, and holiday celebrations. This family values books and travel. They have the wherewithal to provide money and invest time to maximize their child's potential.

Not every child is this fortunate. This is not to say there is fault involved. A child born into poverty or with a chronic medical condition is not always the product of loveless, inattentive parents. What if the pregnant woman is in an auto accident resulting in a premature birth with complications? What if the mother is in the military, enduring vigorous and rugged living conditions prior to knowing she is pregnant? What of children born in war-torn countries? There are infants born to drug using parents. Children are often born to parents who are reckless and engage in self-endangering behaviors.

Life and death are decided by adults. Abortion, war, homicide, suicide, are not the decisions of children. Many youngsters suffer from the harshness of their environmental conditions during their developmental years. Do not mistake this as condemnation to a troubled and unfulfilled life, because now enters factor three, our unique personality.

Picture Me Perfect

When presented with situations, we all have the right of choice. There are those who must touch the hot stove. They are burned. They are angry at the stove. They go back and do it again, expecting a different outcome. They are burned and again blame the stove. They are outraged. They are hurt and believe it wasn't their fault. They are angry, often strike out, retaliate against others, and feel justified in doing so.

You shake your head in amazement, bewildered. You ask, *When will they learn? How can they be so foolish? Why don't they ever listen? What will it take for them to understand?* The answer is that no one is ready to understand until he is ready.

Perhaps you remember the adage, *You cannot put an old head on young shoulders.* Most of us take advantage of the wisdom of others. When they speak, we listen. We consider the options, explore possible alternatives, and weigh positive and negative outcomes. We can learn from the mistakes and experiences of others, without having to endure the events ourselves.

After all, must all drug counselors have been drug users? Must all obstetricians have given birth? Must all music lovers have been musicians? No, but they can teach, explain, and behave in ways that help us learn if we are open to it. *When the student is ready, the teacher arrives.*

There is the child who, despite warnings, chases the bumblebee. Loved ones forewarn, admonish, and run interference, to no avail. They wait for the ultimate outcome. The child succeeds in catching the bumblebee and gets stung. Some will respond to the child with comfort, support, and acceptance. Others will respond with blame, anger, and rejection. Sometimes the response of others helps us do better in our life, sometimes it does not. Some people in life may present a good example, others a bad experience. Either way, we learn from those in our environment.

Our thoughts and feelings lead to our behavior and this is the essence of our unique personality traits. Each of us has a personal worldview. This encompasses how we assess events in our lives and the world at large. It also includes how we react and respond within our environment.

If you were able to write the perfect life script for yourself, what would it look like? What do you value the most? Some possibilities are health, security, wealth, loving relationships, or career success. Name the things that are most important to you and why.

As an example, let's choose money and relationships as two things that you value. Your list may look similar to this:

1. Money
    - Have a steady, permanent
      income

- Be financially secure
- Live comfortably
- Be considered "well off"
- Build wealth
- Give to others

2. Relationships
    - Find my soul mate
    - Have many friends
    - Have close friends
    - Be popular
    - Be loved by many
    - Find acceptance

Once you know what you want and need, you can make a plan to have these things in your life to find success, happiness, and peace.

Some Like It Hot

Whatever decisions were made in your environment took you in one direction or another. Whatever your physical or mental abilities, whatever your limitations, whatever adversity you faced, you developed coping strategies to survive within your environment. You strove to adapt your beliefs and behaviors to "fit" within the reality of your world. You did the best you could with what you had at that time in your life.

Sometimes survival is difficult. At times, we must become "insane" to survive in an "insane world." This is experienced in traumatic situations such as war, prison, and disasters. Children growing up in an environment which involves abuse, addiction, or mental illness, may also feel like a separation of self from reality, a dissociation. Sometimes, you must learn maladaptive behaviors to survive within chaotic family circumstances. This is evident in children of alcoholics and those who have been physically, verbally, emotionally, or sexually abused.

There are children born into financially secure, well-educated families, loved and care for, but somehow reach adulthood as wrong doers. There are youngsters born into poverty, suffering in harsh family situations, yet, as adults become productive, loving, tax-paying citizens. How does this happen? The twists and turns of each individual are based in part on their unique personality traits.

I Will Survive

Over time, our perception of our personal history may change. This may be based on new life experiences or a better understanding of our past. With a change in our thoughts, we feel differently, and this leads to changes in our behavior. As we grow and change, there is always hope of a new and better life.

Children must adapt to survive, regardless of their environment or DNA. Each of us develops a unique personality. Experienced teachers, medical providers, and law enforcement easily identify children with atypical behaviors. The child may have poor physical development, slow learning patterns, or severe behavior problems. Authority figures see these as "flashing red lights" that warn of danger for the developing child. Sadly, the child does not have the benefit of this objective view.

As children, we develop beliefs, emotions, and behaviors based on survival. We learn to adapt ourselves to our environment and do whatever we must in that moment to protect ourselves and survive, whether physically or emotionally.

As we experience life, we model the behavior of others. We also learn by trial and error. We modify our actions based on our beliefs and the consequences we endure. We can adapt and change, but it is difficult because we build up defenses to protect ourselves and survive within our environment.

Perhaps you have never learned positive relationship skills and your experiences with others have been painful. You are blinded by your habitual behaviors and have no reason to seek a solution to a problem you don't think you have. Instead, you put in place an intricate set of defenses to protect your emotional self. These psychological defenses include: denial, projection of blame, and rationalization.

Use of Denial

Picture a child with crumbs on his face standing next to an empty cookie jar. When asked why he took the cookies, he denies ever seeing the cookies, let alone eating them, despite evidence to the contrary. As an adult, when stopped for speeding, this person would blatantly state he was not exceeding the speed limit and the police officer must be mistaken.

These people can't understand why everyone is picking on them and feel others are out to get them. This belief leads to a cynical mindset of, "get them before they get me." They are defensive, with a "chip on their shoulder" attitude. They have an inability to trust others and communication is poor. They build walls to fend off criticism and insulate themselves from feedback they do not want to hear. They befriend only those who agree with them. Individuals who deny their own behavior are the victims, sad sacks, whiners, and complainers of the world.

Projection of Blame

A different emotional defense is projection of blame. Look again at the child standing near the cookie jar. The child may admit he took the cookies, but states it wasn't his fault. His brother told him to take them; a friend gave them to him; you said he could have them. Somehow, he is innocent and someone else is guilty. A famous comedian, Flip Wilson, had a one-liner for this situation: *The devil made me do it!*

As an adult, this person will admit to the police officer he was speeding, but argue there were no posted signs, four other cars going much faster just passed him, and there is no reason for such a low speed limit on this street.

This type of individual seeks to justify his behavior while finding fault with others. He becomes the steamroller, talking louder and longer, arguing to prove he is right and the rest of the world is wrong. He demands proof, evidence, and at least ten good reasons for every thing. This is the essence of the criminal mentality, which blames the victim, the system, or any other scapegoat for his wrong doings.

Rationalization

A more sophisticated technique justifies behavior by making it seem rational, logical, and even beneficial. Let's go back to the cookie jar scenario. The child will admit he ate the cookies, but tell you they were old and stale and he didn't think anyone would want them. He tries to convince you he did you a favor by eating them before the ants got to them. As an adult, he tells the police officer he was just keeping up with the flow of traffic. After all, he didn't want to create a road hazard.

This individual is a manipulator. He is able to use logic and is skilled at putting a small bit of truth in every statement, making it difficult to disagree with him. He attempts to control people with emotional blackmail such as guilt, shame, or blame. There is no winning with this person. After an encounter with him, you come away with self-doubt, feeling frustrated and used.

Your Inner Story

We filter our experiences through our perceptions. Despite how we behave or how others respond to us, we hold a firm worldview and mold events to fit within it. We often misconstrue reality. We find some kernel of truth and tenaciously hold on to it to support our beliefs, feelings, and behaviors. We tend to associate with others who validate our feelings, confirm our beliefs, and sanction our actions.

We create an inner dialogue based on our concept of reality and our personal perception of events. We tell ourselves how we feel—proud, confident, weak, or shy. We set up expectations for ourselves in given situations and often verbalize them. Our words and behaviors tell others how to treat us and what to expect from us.

At times, we advertise our perceived shortcomings. We tell the host we would love to help out, but we're so clumsy, we'll probably drop something. During a job interview, we say we're slow to catch on, but we'll try hard. Self-assured individuals do not point out their weaknesses. They focus on their strengths. Confident individuals don't *try* to do something, they *do* it. Socially secure people don't say they'll think about things, they make a commitment and follow up with action.

We teach others how to treat us. Let me use the lesson of the *Crying Baby*. Even infants learn to control their environment and the people in it to meet their needs. Every mother comes to understand her baby's cry for food, which is different from his cry for attention, or his cry due a bellyache. Those of us blessed with a newborn who cried long into the night can attest to the fact that the volume, tone, and length of our child's cry sent a different message.

As the infant cried, you soothed, fed, burped, changed, and rocked, but the wailing continued. You dressed and undressed. You warmed the milk or cooled the juice. You cradled the babe as you stood in the garage or on the porch. You took the child to sleep in another room to avoid disturbing family members. You walked through darkened rooms and down long hallways. You entertained with toys, you sang, you read. You pushed the stroller on darkened streets. You took long drives to nowhere. The infant cried until dawn, then exhausted, peacefully drifted off into blessed sleep while you struggled to stay awake through the day. That innocent babe found a way to have you to himself all night.

Unfortunately, your day must go on without benefit of sleep. You have to prepare breakfast, pack lunches, check homework, get dressed, drop off children, and bring that precious, sleeping baby to day care so you can go to work. You may also have to schedule a medical appointment for the baby—just in case.

The lesson of the *Crying Baby*? We teach others how to treat us. We control others by our behavior.

You may find yourself asking how you got to this place in your life. The answer? You made choices. You behaved based on your thoughts and emotions. Your actions taught others how to respond to you—how to treat you. You made decisions and brought yourself to where you are today.

~ *Keep learning new things* ~

Chapter 3

You Got Yourself There, You Can Get Yourself Back

Decisions, Decisions, Decisions

You may make a good decision, which may have a bad outcome. Does that mean you made a terrible decision? Not necessarily, yet you judge yourself not on the decision, but on the result.

Why do you worry about making decisions? You worry because it may not turn out "right." You may make a mistake and then what would happen? What would people think? What would they say? You may be blamed, you may feel guilty, and you may feel foolish. Sometimes we avoid making decisions based on these emotional issues.

Life is not static, it is fluid. It ebbs and flows. You grow and change as you move through life. Before you went to school, you stayed home. Before you graduated, you were in school. Before you married, you were single. Before you got your first job, you were unemployed. Before your final career, you had other jobs. Before retirement you worked. Before you lived here, you lived somewhere else.

All of these changes came about because you made decisions. Confronted with situations or events you considered alternatives and made choices. At times, you may have had to choose between two negative possibilities, but there was no escape from making a choice.

There is an old story of a man facing his executioner.

"Do you want to be shot or do you want to be hung?" the executioner asked.

The man replied, "I don't want to die."

The executioner simply said, "That Sir, is not one of your choices."

Sometimes, during the course of life, you may feel the only choices you have are between negative alternatives —bad and worse. There is no such thing as not choosing.

Not choosing is itself a choice. Indecision is a heavy burden, which saps our emotional strength. You waiver, question yourself, become overwhelmed, and procrastinate. When this happens, you have decided to sit back and become passive. You have become reactive instead of proactive in your life.

We always make a decision. We decide to be active or reactive. In the active decision mode, you take charge and become proactive in your life. You make the choice. You put yourself in the driver's seat. Even if the vehicle is out of control, you take charge of the situation and mitigate the outcome.

In the reactive decision mode, you allow others to decide and you react to their choice. You are in the passenger seat. If the vehicle is careening out of control, you are a captive victim.

You may think others or circumstances have dealt you a bad hand. This is certainly true in some situations, but it's up to you to play the hand you were dealt to your best advantage. It's not that unfortunate things haven't happened or won't happen again; it's how you work through these events that lead to feelings of satisfaction, success, and self-efficacy. Facing and overcoming the perils of life leads to feelings of self-worth and builds self-confidence. How we handle adversity determines the quality of our life.

Good Decisions, Bad Outcomes

As always, we do the best we can with what we have at that moment in time. When faced with various life situations, we consider options and make choices. If the outcome is good, we feel good. If it turns out bad, we feel bad. Often we beat ourselves up about a bad decision, when in fact we made a good decision that happened to have a bad outcome. However, the outcome was not necessarily the result of a poor decision on our part.

Let me explain with this example. Let's consider your decision to purchase a new car or to keep the one you have. You may reason your current vehicle is old and undependable. You have spent a lot of money on repairs. You worry about your safety or what may go wrong with the car next. Another part of you thinks, this car is old, but it's paid for. You've replaced everything on it. What else could go wrong?

You consider the new car purchase. The price is right, the payments affordable, and the dealer is willing to give you a good trade-in price on your current vehicle. The new car has an extended warranty, improved safety features, and better mileage. Besides, you work hard and deserve to enjoy the fruits of your labor.

After consideration of all the options, you decide to purchase the new car. You believe you have made a sound decision. Let's say the next week you get a promotion at work, with a hefty pay raise. Now you feel even better about your decision to buy the new car because the financial burden is lessened.

About two weeks later a family member becomes ill and has no insurance to pay for medical care. Your employer calls a meeting to discuss a reduction-in-staff. Your partner has to cut back on his or her hours at work. The roof starts to leak and you're sure you spied termites clustering around the wood frame over the garage door. Now you start to feel bad about your decision to buy the new car because you can't afford it.

Did you really make a poor decision when you purchased the new car? We tend to judge ourselves by the outcome of our decisions, which is unfair. When making a decision, we don't know the outcome. Without a crystal ball, we can only consider options and plan for a good outcome, but we cannot predict it with certainty.

We beat ourselves up about a good decision because it had a bad result. The decision wasn't bad; the outcome was unpredictable at the time the decision was made.

Given the car purchase scenario, obviously neither outcome—your good fortune at work nor the misfortune of family illness—occurred before your decision to purchase the car. You made the decision based on the information you had at the time. You did make a sound decision. Events after the fact now influence how you feel about the decision you made. This does not make sense.

We cannot predict what will come next in life. We make decisions based on the information we have at hand, the benefit of experience, and a reasonable prediction of outcomes.

If the outcome of our decision is less than desirable, we need to develop a new plan based on the new information and circumstances. Again, we will make a decision based on what we now know. This is a process of evaluating a situation, considering options, making choices, and re-evaluating. Do not blame or criticize yourself for unforeseeable outcomes.

What is the Worst Thing That Can Happen?

When considering change always think of the worse thing that could happen. Rarely are any of our decisions life threatening or irrevocable. What if you do create a disaster?

You may feel foolish, embarrassed, guilty, worried, or angry. You imagine a catastrophe and perceive negative, life-long repercussions. *This is the worst moment of my life. It's all over for me now. I'll never be able to face these people again. I'll definitely lose my job over this. My family will never forgive me.*

Are you really that important? Are your actions so powerful they will alter the course of history? Unlikely. If there is a serious negative outcome because of your poor decision or bad behavior, take responsibility, make amends, and learn something. Unburden yourself from guilt. Understand you are human, forgive yourself, and move on with your life.

The More We Learn, the Better We Do

Every day, we are faced with decisions, big and small. Should you cook or go out to eat? Should you paint the walls tan or blue? Should you stop on the way home to buy milk? Should you stay in school or not? Should you go to college? Should you join the military or seek employment? Should you get married now or wait months?

There are things you did or didn't do which moved you in one direction or another in life. At the fork in the road, you went right or left, and that decision, and all that followed, led you to where you are today.

Without the ability to see into the future, we make decisions in real time, and we usually make good decisions. Unfortunately, we have no control over all the variables which may affect the outcome. We learn from our decisions, good and bad, and the more we learn, the better we do.

Negativity is Beating You Up

We often berate ourselves after the fact. We tear ourselves apart for making a bad decision, or using poor judgment. This is akin to the Monday morning quarterback. After the event, when we have time to review, reconsider, and take in new information, we realize we should have made a different decision. However, we make decisions based on what we know at the time, not on what happens later.

We are quick to spotlight our shortcomings in these situations. We beat ourselves up and not just about the immediate situation, but we recall other past failures.

Remember when you lost the spelling bee in third grade? Remember when you fell off your bike and ripped your new pants? What about that first date disaster? What went on during that confusing job interview? How about those unkind remarks you made that were overhead by the target of your gossip?

Ah, you are such a bad, mean, inconsiderate person! If you don't believe it, just listen to yourself. You are tearing yourself apart with feelings of shame, blame, and guilt. You have become punitive, belittling yourself. You are lowering your self-esteem and undermining your confidence.

Why are you doing this to yourself? Why are you so harsh? Why do you demean yourself? The key word is *YOU*. You are doing this to yourself. If others spoke to you like this, or treated you this way, understandably, you would be upset.

You would be insulted and not consider this person among your friends. Are you a good friend to yourself?

You do not need to feel bad about or disappointed in yourself. Accept responsibility for your decisions and the consequences. This is a growth experience. Keep it in perspective and it will lead to better decision making the next time. Give yourself permission to make mistakes.

When you set up a negative scenario of self-criticism, you are not your friend. You are sending a message to yourself and others that you are a worthless person. You have become your enemy.

Kick Me, Please

They say it pays to advertise. What do you tell others about yourself? *I'm a klutz. I'm not good at math. I cant' walk and chew gum at the same time. I've always been overweight. I'll never win any beauty contest. I never get things done. I just can't keep a job. I'm not as smart as others.*

Would you like to hear others say these things about you? No? Then why talk about yourself this way?

You have strengths and talents, areas in which you excel. This means there are other areas in which you are not as accomplished. It does not mean weakness or failure. You need to focus on those things you do well. Realize, with learning and practice, there are many areas where you could find success, if you chose to put in the time and effort. After all, what is a weed, but a plant whose virtues have yet to be discovered?

You must be realistic and put things in perspective. Suppose you had a Ph.D. in finance. Do you think you could perform a root canal? How about brain surgery? After all, you are obviously intelligent and well educated. What's the problem? You may be an outstanding accountant, but doing a root canal or brain surgery is not your area of expertise. It doesn't mean you couldn't do it. It means you do not have the education, experience, or interest in doing it.

This same reasoning holds true for repairing your car, baking pies, using the computer, or playing the piano. You're better at some things than others. Start advertising your strengths.

Write Your Own Script

Forget what you've been told; write your own script. The self-fulfilling prophecy is alive and well in life and it can work positively or negatively.

A positive life script could have developed in this manner. You received messages of love, encouragement, and support with expectations of success.

Let's use athletics as an example. As a young child, you were told how strong you were, what big muscles you had, and how coordinated you were.

Baby stories told with pride relayed how you walked early, rode your two-wheeled bike before starting Kindergarten, and did cartwheels on your seventh birthday. You were a natural in T-ball. Photos taken at every sporting event were proudly displayed, and sent to friends and relatives. When the time came for you to start high school, the expectation was you would join the soccer team and likely be the MVP. If you were injured, it was viewed as a bump in the road to be overcome quickly, so you could continue to move up and on to greatness. You adopted and internalized this self-view as a competent and successful athlete.

As an adult, you continued to work out or jog three times a week. You befriended and associated with people who also enjoyed fitness activities. Your partner and coworkers commented on your lean physique, muscular build, broad shoulders, or small waist. You were motivated to fulfill and maintain your belief and reputation as a healthy, active, athletic person throughout the course of your life and into old age.

This positive outlook was presented to you as a young child. It was perpetuated throughout your life by your own words and actions, which sent a positive message to others, who in turn reinforced your belief.

Surely, as a child, you fell off your bike, missed the pitched ball, or didn't make first string. These experiences were considered an exception to your usual performance. You were not punished or berated. You were encouraged to do better, urged to learn from it, and move on. These positive experiences, in a supportive environment, were internalized by you and created a positive self-fulfilling prophecy.

Sadly, a negative life script could have developed taking you and your worldview in a different direction. Acceptance and support from significant others in your life may have been offered with contingencies. Your life could have been based on "if/than" rather than on "unconditional regard." You may have struggled for recognition based on performance. The message you received could have been one of worthlessness and rejection.

As a young child, you may have been criticized when you tried anything new, especially if it did not have a successful outcome. Any misstep became an opportunity for criticism, shame, and blame. You were ridiculed when you fell off the two-wheeled bike. You were teased about your appearance. You were mocked for your grades in school. You became shy and grew up afraid and discouraged. New situations aroused anxiety and feelings of failure. You felt defeated before you began. You may have learned to approach life with trepidation and the expectation of failure or harm.

As an adult, in an effort to avoid judgment, you hesitated to be around others. You faded into the background at your place of employment to avoid criticism. You minimized your accomplishments and belittled yourself. You felt inadequate compared to your peers—personally, socially, financially, and vocationally. You sent these negative messages directly and indirectly to others and they obliged you by accepting them as true.

This negative personal assessment has been delivered to you since childhood. You have internalized it and now perpetuate it through your own words and actions. You tell others you're not sure you can finish the project on time. You tell your family you may never have enough money for financial security. You tell people life is too hard and the world is a dangerous place.

You have assumed the *victim* position and expect to engage in lose-lose situations. You feel defeated. You anticipate others taking advantage of you. Your negative self-image is firmly entrenched. You not only believe you are inept and incapable, but you offer that message to all those you meet. You may not have created your negative self-image, but you are supporting it and playing out your own negative self-fulfilling prophecy.

Our day-to-day lives may reflect the quote attributed to Job, "That which I greatly fear, has come upon me." Whether positive or negative, that which we firmly believe, will surely come true.

~ Hang in there ~

Chapter 4

It's Not What You Say, It's What You Do That Counts

Work Your Plan

If you want something you've never had before, you must do something you've never done before. It is not enough to say you will do something; you must actually do it. You must be motivated. You must set a goal, create a plan, and take action.

Here is an example. Have you ever disappointed someone by forgetting his or her birthday? How many excuses did you make?

- *It's easy to forget when it only comes once a year.*
- *I was sooooo busy.*

- *I was thinking about you, but forgot to call.*
- *It's not that big of a deal.*
- *You are way too sensitive!*
- *I'll make it up to you.*

Let's make a comparison. Suppose you had a winning lotto ticket worth 5 million dollars. Let's say there is only one day in the year you can redeem that ticket.

Would you forget which day is was? Would you be too busy? What would you do to remind yourself to redeem that ticket on that day? Do you think you would forget? Unlikely. Why? That winning ticket has become the most important thing in your life.

You are focused and committed to remember that date. You will make every arrangement, accommodation, and preparation to go wherever and do whatever to cash in that ticket. You will design a back-up plan for that date, just in case something goes amiss. You are fully committed and motivated. Nothing will hold you back.

That winning ticket will change your life!

Is your friend, spouse, parent, sibling or child less important? Have they not made a significant change in your life?

Action is a matter of motivation. You must perceive a person or event as important. It has to have significance for you. You *can* take action. The question is—*will* you?

Dilly-Dallying Along the Way

We all know the "promise breakers." They tell you anything then do what they want. You talk, you discuss, you negotiate, and you compromise. You think you have established a meeting of the minds, based on trust and understanding. A mutual decision has been made and agreed upon. You are invested in this person and your relationship.

This is exactly why we are not just disappointed, but devastated, when those we love let us down. It is not just disappointment, but also the violation of trust that leaves us feeling used. We are hurt when someone we trust treats us badly and we are angry we allowed it to happen. What we perceive as trust they perceive as weakness.

We all have a tolerance level; beyond which we will not go. We have needs and wants; we have our own agenda in life. Whether it is husband and wife, parent and child, neighbor and friend, or employer and employee, we form relationships to meet our mutual needs. At times, we support others and at times, they support us, but for the most part, we stand on our own, seeking love, acceptance, comfort, belonging, and security from others.

When our needs are no longer met, the essence of the relationship is over. We may not formally end it by quitting our job, leaving home, or getting divorced, but the essence of the relationship has been lost. We are now dragging a "dead horse" and it is making us weary.

Who's Crying Now?

It is a matter of personal integrity to keep your word, to be dependable and responsible. Do you frustrate friends or coworkers by being chronically late or disorganized? Do you make promises you don't keep?

When you don't keep your word, you lack integrity. The message you send is that you are the only important one in the relationship. The other person doesn't matter.

To earn the reputation as one who never does what he says, detracts from your character and quality of life. Others do not respect you nor hold you in high regard. The message you send is they are not important to you. Slowly, you will come to realize you are no longer important to them. This belief has become mutual.

The more you engage in making excuses—*I forgot. Why didn't you remind me? I wrote it in my planner—* the more you chip away at your integrity. When your words are not followed by actions, trust and respect are lost. Relationships are damaged, not because we lack ability. Relationships are lost because we lack motivation, we are undependable and unwilling to do what we say we will do.

How Do I Love Thee?

When you cannot depend on someone to be honest, loyal, or responsible, the relationship begins to fall apart. You become apprehensive. You have self-doubts.

If your needs aren't being met and the relationship is creating negative emotions, you must take charge. Are you being realistic? Are your demands excessive? Have you shifted responsibility for meeting your needs onto someone else? Have you created a plan for failure? We must realistically assess our emotional needs, before we blame others for not meeting them.

Think, Feel, Act

Behavior is a three-step process. We think, we feel, and then we act. Understand, we feel and act on what we perceive to be true, not necessarily what is true. At times, reality and perception are misaligned.

For example, suppose you hear sirens in the distance. The sound is getting louder. Emergency vehicles are approaching your home. Thinking there is an accident or urgent situation nearby, you begin to feel anxious. You go outside and look around, soon you run to the end of your street for a better look. Now, the sirens fade as emergency vehicles move away from your home and onto the highway.

Neighbors may see you running and wonder what you are doing. When approached and questioned you feel foolish. Your behavior was not based on *reality*—there was a need for emergency services some distance away. Your behavior was based on your *perception* of reality—the danger was close to your home and you needed to respond. You behaved based on your perception of the circumstances not the reality of the circumstances.

This is how we react to life events. We assess a situation, as we understand it at that moment in time. We consider alternatives and weigh benefits and risks. We behave based on what we believe is happening and how we feel at that moment. All of this can happen in a matter of seconds.

We think, we feel, and then we act. This may seem instantaneous, but it is three separate steps. The key is our perception, not necessarily reality. Perception is our understanding of reality at that moment. Our perception may or may not reflect what is actually happening. This is often the basis for misunderstandings.

Misperception Leads to Miscommunication

People are often hurt or angered by the behavior of others. They may be so stunned or overwhelmed they do not take time to communicate. However, the misdeed may be unintended and based on a misinterpretation of reality.

Some years ago a couple in a car was cut off in traffic by another vehicle. The first car pulled into a gas station, the second car followed. The driver of the first vehicle, feeling intimidated and prompted by his female passenger armed himself with a knife and approached the second car. The driver of the second car, feeling threatened, put up a struggle and was fatally stabbed. The driver of the first car was arrested.

During the trial, it was discovered the second vehicle was not the offending car which cut them off. Horrified by this turn of events, the accused and his female passenger committed suicide. This tragedy was triggered by a careless act, which lead to a mutual misunderstanding and a lack of verbal communication.

Thoughts and feelings were not given a *reality check* prior to taking action. In the heat of the moment, behavior was based on what each person thought to be true leading to a violent outcome for all involved.

Assertive vs. Aggressive

We have an obligation to be open to the possibility that actions do not always have ill intent. We also have an obligation to communicate with others in an assertive manner. This involves stating our needs, our understanding of what has occurred, and how we feel about it. This allows the other person an opportunity to discuss and explain his actions without shame, blame, or guilt. How we respond in these situations can clarify, minimize, or resolve our emotional responses and the behaviors that follow.

Being assertive is not the same as being aggressive. Think of assertiveness as two adults having an objective conversation to assess a situation or event. They are not bringing their emotions to the forefront. They are not seeking to find fault, place blame, or assume ill will.

Assertiveness is making a statement without feeling defensive or offering proof for one's thoughts, feelings, actions, or point of view. Assertiveness is not threatening nor is it submissive. An assertive individual has self-awareness and self-confidence. He is willing and able to establish personal boundaries. He does not fear stating his opinions or feelings openly. He is not concerned with trying to influence others. He is willing to respect the personal opinions of others and defend himself against aggressiveness.

Assertive communication strives to fulfill needs and wants through cooperation. Assertiveness results in understanding but does not require agreement.

Aggression is a hostile activity, often unprovoked. Aggression can be verbal, physical, or emotional. It is based in anger and used defensively. Aggression assumes ill will, blame, and fault. It results in criticism, insults, and confrontations. It is used to intimidate, bully, or threaten others. Aggressive communication strives to impose one's belief and/or behavior on others. Aggression demands agreement with the aggressor and implies harm will occur on some level if it doesn't happen.

He Did It On Purpose

Behavior is purposeful, it meets our needs. Our actions have primary and secondary gains. For example, if you decide to attend college you obtain a formal education. It opens doors of opportunity, broadens employment options, and increases your earning potential. It may extend your social contacts. These are primary gains.

However, there are also secondary gains. Perhaps while you attend college, others pay your bills. Expectations of family involvement may be minimal because you have to attend class and need time to study. As long as you are in college, you don't have to face decisions about finding a job, choosing a career, or earning a living. You are relieved of certain responsibilities. Others may make fewer demands on you. These are secondary gains.

Before you demand that others change, understand their needs. What are they gaining by their behavior? What are the primary and secondary gains? When you understand these issues, you will know why they are unwilling to change. When frustrated by another's behavior, take time to ask yourself these questions:

- What would I gain if he or she changed?
- How would these changes meet my needs?

- What can I do to meet my own needs?

For example, let's say you and your partner disagree on spending money. You want him to be more cautious and put money into savings. He feels he works hard and should buy whatever he wants. One of you feels you need more income, the other feels you need to spend more wisely.

Ask yourself:

Q. What would I gain if he changed?
A.   Mutual agreement regarding purchases, money for emergencies, funds for retirement, less arguing, better communication, more trust.

Q. How would these changes meet my needs?
A. I would feel financially secure. I would feel he respects by opinion.

Q. What can I do to meet my own needs?

A. Get a job, get a second job, change jobs, work overtime, learn new skills for higher pay, save regularly, use direct deposit, have automatic deductions into savings, spend less, use coupons, reduce debt, reduce interest on debt.

Your answers will vary depending on your circumstances. You can generate alternatives and consider choices once you have identified your needs. Some solutions will be more acceptable to you than others. If you are uncomfortable with the choices you face, realistically assess your situation. You may need to reevaluate the demands you are making on others. You cannot expect someone else to change to meet your needs. You must take charge of your life. You must make the changes. You must meet your own needs.

What if you both agree on a plan, but only one of you follows it. Resentment builds, arguments ensue, communication breaks down, lies are told, and cover-ups are made. Trust erodes and the relationship falters. Although both agreed on the plan, it didn't work because one partner didn't do what was agreed upon. His or her actions didn't reflect the words that were spoken.

~ Light just one little candle ~

Chapter 5

You Cannot Change Someone Else

If Only

You can allow your life to come to a screeching halt with a severe case of the *If Only Syndrome*. It goes something like this:

If only...
- He loved me
- My children called more often
- I was treated with respect
- He wouldn't be so mean
- She would stay in school
- They would pay me what I am worth
- People would care about me
- He would stop drinking
- She would stop overspending

The common pattern in the *If Only Syndrome* is your finger is pointing toward others instead of toward you. When stuck in the *If Only* state of mind, you try to change someone else. Stop. Give it up. It doesn't work. No one can change someone else.

What we can do is change ourselves. We can explore what we want and need. We can set goals and take action to meet our own needs. We can stop holding others accountable for what we want, including our happiness. Others do not prevent us from having what we want. We do that ourselves.

We may be able to influence others with our behavior. We can take a stand for our values and stay true to ourselves. We can be part of the solution rather than part of the problem. We can do what we believe is the right thing or we can be a bad example. This may have an influence on others, but we cannot change them. It's their job to change themselves.

I Am So Right and You Are So Wrong

Understand, the issue is not who's right and who's wrong. For example, most would agree education is a good thing. Those who stay in school tend to have better opportunities, earn more money, and have a higher standard of living. Are we wrong when we tell a teenager to stay in school? No, but unless the youngster is willing to do so, our saying it won't put him in the classroom, seated at his desk, reading his textbook.

We know when someone has been drinking heavily, he should not get in a car and drive. Read the statistics about fatalities related to alcohol consumption. Thousands of people sustain severe and life altering injuries due to auto accidents where alcohol is involved. Lives are changed in an instant. Sometimes, the innocent party is forever damaged by the reckless decision of another.

We are not wrong when we warn others not to drink and drive. However, it takes more than our admonishments to get another person to put down his drink and hand over his car keys. We are right, but we cannot make another person conform to our demands. That is the job of law enforcement.

The reality is we cannot change others, no matter how right we are or how wrong they are. If making others change was a simple matter of getting them to follow good advice, the world would be a better place. Everyone would graduate from high school, jails and prisons would be unnecessary, there would be no traffic jams, and no one would have cavities. Unfortunately, being right does not provide motivation for others to do right.

Conflict arises when we begin to demand validation from others that we are right and they are wrong. Remember, it's not what he does, it's what you do that counts. Demanding that others change is a losing proposition. It turns us into a person we don't want to be: nagging, scolding, reminding, and warning. We wear ourselves out with the same refrain. *See what happens? You'll be sorry. You won't stop until something goes wrong. Why can't you just follow the rules? Can't you see what you're doing? You know I'm right!*

We become frustrated with our inability to force change onto someone else, especially when we know we are right. Our feeling of helplessness frustrates us. They boldly resist our intervention, relationships fall apart, and still their negative behaviors continue.

Stop That! It's Bad for You

When we put our full effort into trying to change someone else to improve our life, it's likely time to peek inside ourselves. Most of us are not merely being selfish when we try to force others to change. We realize the negative impact their behavior has on them as well as on others including us. Behavior is like a stone thrown into the water, with the ripples going out forever from the point of impact.

Consider your perspective of an individual's behavior and how it touches the lives of others, directly or indirectly. This may involve legal or financial matters. Health and safety may be an issue, especially if young children, dependent adults, or pets are involved. It's easy to decide what others should or should not do. It's more difficult to determine what we need to do or stop doing to bring about change.

Smoking is an interesting example of people not taking good advice. Scientists and medical experts have given severe warnings that smoking causes illness and death. Most smokers admit knowing this, yet they continue to light up. Smoking doesn't seem to have any redeeming features, but thousands of people smoke each day.

Smoking is very colorful: yellow teeth, orange fingertips, and black lungs. The monetary cost is high not just for the purchase, but destruction of property, house fires, lost wages, and high medical expenses. Demanding the smoker quit, is offering a solution to a problem the smoker doesn't think he has. This is oh, so frustrating for us!

Here is another sad, but common example. If your adult son is intoxicated and intends to drive, you can attempt to dissuade him verbally. This might be enough to redirect him. If not, what are your other options?

You can continue to nag or yell which may result in an argument, but is unlikely to keep him from driving. You can explain the possible negative outcomes of his behavior: Suppose he has an accident. What if he has passengers? What about the safety of pedestrians or other drivers on the road? What about the legal ramifications?

You can attempt to confiscate the car keys. This could lead to a confrontation, verbal assault, or physical battery. You could call the authorities and let them handle it. This may or may not actually prevent your son from driving while intoxicated. It could make matters worse. What if your son takes off before the police arrive? What if a car chase ensues? What if he gets into an accident and he or others are injured or killed? What if he resists law enforcement authorities?

You have now hit a rough place in the road. You've been put in a situation you did not create, yet are forced to deal with. There is no good choice. If you allow an intoxicated individual to drive, you may feel guilty, angry, and frustrated. You become deeply concerned about safety and legal issues. If you contact the authorities, it could lead to a worse situation. What will happen to the relationship between you and your son? To add insult to injury, others may point the finger at you as an inept parent or an outright troublemaker.

In these situations, we seek balance between *possible risk* and *probable risk*. If the *possible risk* is low, we tend to take the "wait and see" approach and thus avoid confrontation and negativity. Our concern is that we are over reacting or making a bad situation worse. If the *probable risk* is high, we are more likely to take a stronger stance regardless of the reaction of others. Our thinking is that the certain outcome of our interference is less troublesome than the likely outcome of their dangerous behavior.

However we respond takes a toll on us physically and emotionally. We worry, experience stress, and endure high anxiety. We're exhausted and may experience somatic complaints such as stomach upset, vague pains, or headache.

In these situations, we tap into an inner strength that guides us in the right direction. Some call this a sixth sense, a gut reaction, or an inner voice.

We know what we should do. Somewhere deep within each of us is a moral compass that acts as a guiding force. The further we stray from our inner ethical and moral values, the more uneasy we feel. This inner conflict pushes and pulls, leaving us emotionally drained and frustrated. We are forced to deal with an upsetting situation we did not create and to endure the consequences we don't deserve.

Shout it From the Housetop

You have a right to your opinions and emotions. There are times when you not only have a right, but an obligation to voice your opinions. It's wise to offer advice and information when you clearly see someone making a poor decision.

Does this mean they will take your advice? Will they drop everything, make an about-face, and change instantaneously? Unlikely, but should this stop you from saying what you feel is right? No. You have a right to think and feel as you do, however, you do not have the right to force your opinions onto others.

The problem is not your opinion, but your expectation that yours is the only opinion that matters. When you begin to think in absolutes, you create a problem for yourself and others. You will be disappointed and frustrated when others do not see things your way, when they do not do what you want. Remember, it's not a matter of who is right and who's wrong.

Again, what you are doing is offering someone a solution to a problem he doesn't think he has.

If I offered you an aspirin right now, would you take it? *Why not? Here it is, free for your headache. Please take it, don't hurt my feelings.*

Hmm…. Maybe you don't have a headache. Maybe you are allergic to aspirin. Maybe you take some other medication and can't take aspirin along with it. Maybe you resent me trying to read your mind about what is bothering you. Maybe you wish I would stop offering you a solution to a problem you don't think you have.

This is how resentment builds. Others may accuse us of meddling in their business. Are we wrong with our advice? Maybe. Maybe not. Even if we are right and they are wrong, we cannot change them. We have a solution, which they need, but do not want. How frustrating!

We may be able to pressure others into some temporary change, or at least get them to say, *Yes dear,* or *Sure I will*, or *Next time I'll do it that way*. Typically, the motivation for these responses is guilt, shame, or blame. It is never true change. It is an effort to be left alone. It is not a permanent change in their thinking, feelings, or behavior. It is an appeasing gesture, which creates resentment.

They feel forced to agree with us in the moment and as soon as possible will revert to their own choice of behavior. We then become even more frustrated because we thought we had a commitment from them to do as we said. This false reliance makes things worse because now we feel betrayed, let down, and disappointed. We want to believe this person has really changed as a result of our advice. Not true.

Think about it. If we could just say, *Do not drink and drive*, and they handed us the car keys, wouldn't that be great? Do you really think no one

prior to you has asked, begged, or pleaded with this person to get out of the car if he has been drinking? Has it made a difference? Here he is again, alcohol on his breath, approaching his car and you calling after him to stop. Has he really changed?

What of all the parents who have said, *Stay in school,* and *Don't be a drop out.* Probably hundreds of teachers, coaches, and youth leaders have said these words thousands of times. Do we now have a 100% graduation rate? No. Is it because all of those people were wrong? No. It is because we all have the right to make our own decisions, despite good advice from others.

Many people have heard these words of wisdom: *Save for a rainy day.* This is certainly good advice, but is everyone financially secure? No. We may hear, but we do not always listen.

~ Take care of yourself to serve others better ~

Chapter 6

More Than Seven Deadly Sins

The Three "Rs"

The keys to a fulfilling life are respect, responsibility, and resilience. These are the basic ingredients for building and maintaining inner peace.

Respect for others and ourselves is essential. Whether by word or deed, be kind and gentle. We often harm others, even when we speak the truth. Before you speak consider three things. Is it truthful? Is it necessary? Is it harmful?

Although what we say may be truthful, is it necessary? Consider the time and place for your reveal. Will it help or improve the situation? Worse, will it be harmful? Do not say anything you are not willing to put in writing and sign your name to. Remember, there are some things that should go to the grave.

Most responses to life situations are not based on right or wrong, but rather on appropriate or inappropriate. Can you appear at the library or in church in your teeny-tiny bikini? Yes. Is there any law that you cannot dress as you please? No. Is it appropriate? No. It is not *wrong* in an absolute sense, however, it is *wrong* in a moral sense. It is inappropriate because it is offensive and disrespectful to others.

We behave inappropriately in less obvious ways–interrupting others, loud phone conversations in public places, cutting someone off so we can be first in line, or telling those cute growing-up stories in front of your son's new girlfriend.

Sadly, we hit where it hurts. We tease and embarrass others. Our often voiced excuse is, *But it's the truth*. It may well be, but the real issue is our need to feel superior. If we can make someone else look bad or foolish, by comparison, we seem to look better. Shame, shame on you, the bully!

We need to behave responsibly at all times, not just when it is easy or convenient. There are behaviors which, when done to excess are problematic and show a lack of responsibility.

Alcohol is not harmful in moderation. The benefits of red wine are now touted for its healing antioxidant properties. However, drinking to excess has a negative impact on your health and can result in a dangerous or harmful outcome for others.

Drugs can simply be prescribed medication, which keeps thousands of people alive and well. Drugs taken to excess, even if prescribed for a legitimate medical condition, are dangerous. Medications taken by the wrong person or in dosages not prescribed create havoc. Street drugs are unknown chemical compounds with questionable usefulness and always dangerous.

Sex is a biological drive necessary for survival of the species. Intercourse was designed to be pleasurable, to ensure we procreate and continue the species for generations. Sexual activities to the extreme, such as promiscuity, prostitution, sexual assaults, or pedophilia, are dangerous and in some cases criminal.

There are those who are dishonest and weave a tangled web of mistrust. There are sins of commission and sins of omission. A good example is the man who admitted to stealing a rope, however, did not mention there was a horse tied to the other end of it. Did he lie? Yes he did. He didn't tell the whole truth. He omitted the truth. Honesty is a matter of integrity. Honesty is acting responsibly.

It Was That Way When I Got Here

Accepting responsibility for one's behavior is essential for good mental health. As a very young child, we begin to develop a sense of right and wrong. We begin to make decisions based on our environment, temperament, and emerging personality.

For example, a two-year-old in the grocery store will pull a candy from the shelf and proudly tear open the package to show Mom what he can do. At this moment, Mom takes the time to teach the child right from wrong: *This does not belong to us. We must ask permission to have it. We must pay for it. We must give it back.*

When a four year old sees the candy, he will look around and sneak it into his pocket. When found out, he will be punished.

The behavior is essentially the same. The child took something that did not belong to him, however, the intent and outcome are quite different. The two year old is innocent. He is learning right from wrong. His focus is on his emerging skills of independence and fine motor control. He is proud of his accomplishment. By the time the a child is four, he knows right from wrong and consciously makes a choice to do what is right or what is forbidden. This is why the child sneaks to do the deed. He knows it's wrong. It is critical the parent impose a consequence so the child learns behaviors which are acceptable and unacceptable.

Honesty is not based on being caught or punished. The core issue is integrity; knowing right from wrong and choosing to do what is right. As a child, you learned to adapt your behavior to the demands and expectations of others. You learn to cooperate and conform for the greater good. Typically, when you do wrong or cause harm, you empathize with those you hurt and feel sorry and ashamed for your wrongdoing.

When you knowingly do the wrong thing, you feel guilty. This emotion is so powerful and unpleasant, you want to avoid it, and thus will choose to do the right thing. You began to take responsibility for your decisions and actions. You begin to develop a conscience.

Once Upon a Time

Perhaps Mom didn't read you a bed time story. Maybe Dad spanked you when you were being potty trained. If so, it is sad. What happened to you as a child may have caused you physical or emotional suffering. The real tragedy isn't what happened during your childhood, but as an adult you allow the past to control you in negative ways. You can continue to punish yourself, taking over where others left off or you can take charge and make positive changes in your life.

It is essential to take responsibility for your thoughts, words, and actions if you are to find inner peace. Pointing the finger at yourself is not easy; however, you are the only one responsible and entitled to run your life.

Certainly, events happen which are not of your making. You may become ill, people are inconsiderate, someone doesn't like you, and there are "politics" in the workplace. You do not have control over everything that happens, however, you have absolute control over how you respond to what happens.

You can spend your life in denial, blaming others, or finding fault, and at times be justified. The question is not whether you are right or wrong, but how your responses improve your life and well-being.

There are those who are irresponsible. They do not do what is expected of them. When it is brought to their attention, they respond with indignation. They are resentful of others who point out their faults, or criticize them.

Interestingly, it's easy to point out the faults of others. We're quick to identify their shortcomings. We can clearly see how their negative behavior influences our life and is ruining theirs. "If only" is a common theme: *If only... he would be more considerate,...   go to school, get a job,...save money. If only...she would stop drinking,...lose weight,...quit nagging.*

You may be on target and perfectly reasonable in your expectations. The key is, these expectations belong to you, not to the other person. You may know all the things someone else needs to do, to better his life, have more friends, or improve relationships. However, you cannot live someone else's life, solve his problems, nor change his personality. You are not responsible for how someone else thinks, what he says, or how he behaves. You cannot control someone else. You are only responsible for yourself.

Persecute and then Rescue the Victim

Our expectations of others and the demands we place on them often leads to conflict. The fact they didn't put out the garbage, keep a job, or pay the electric bill is now lost in the Victim- Persecutor-Rescuer role-playing. This is known as the Karpman Triangle.

An example is the youngster who brings home a report card with failing grades.

Mom rants over the boy's lack of study habits and criticizes him for not doing his homework.

Mom is the persecutor and the boy is the victim.

When Dad arrives home, he raises his voice and threatens to ground his son for two months.

Dad is now the persecutor, the son is the victim.

The boy protests and accuses his father of not loving him.

The boy is now the persecutor and Dad is the victim.

Mom jumps in and tells the boy not to speak to his father in that tone.

Mom is now the persecutor of the boy and rescuer of Dad.

The boy starts to cry and blames Mom for picking on him.

The son is now the persecutor and Mom is the victim.

Dad defends the boy—after all, he is just a child, no need to be so harsh.

Dad is now the rescuer of the boy. He has also become the persecutor of Mom.

Mom now raises her voice to Dad and is critical of him for making excuses for their son.

Mom has now become the persecutor. Dad has become the victim.

The son now tells Mom to leave Dad alone. *The son has now become the rescuer of Dad and Mom has become his victim.*

This race of emotions around the Victim-Persecutor-Rescuer triangle can happen within a matter of seconds, but the backlash can last a lifetime. All involved feel they have been mistreated. There is nothing positive in this type of interaction. It only results in negativity.

There are those who endanger themselves and others by their irresponsible decisions and reckless behaviors. This is often seen in the parent-child relationship during the teenage years.

The youngster refuses to attend school, shoplifts, or drives without a license. Not only does the teen not have a consequence, but his or her parents are held accountable morally, financially, and legally. The youngster often has no empathy for those he has harmed. He also ignores the damage he has caused within the family relationship.

Will they ever learn? Maybe. Maybe not. We can offer guidance, but we cannot change someone else. At best, we become the *gatekeeper*. We strive to direct, monitor, and protect others. Sometimes this is successful.

Sometimes it is not. We are only responsible for our own words and deeds, not that of others.

It's Your Turn to Call

Many relationships fall apart because we avoid the responsibility of communication. Everything we do and don't do, say and don't say, sends a message to those around us.

If your verbal skills are poor or you refuse to speak to others because you are withdrawn, angry, or hurt, the relationship suffers. You force others to attempt to read your mind. A typical example happens every day in thousands of homes.

He: *What's wrong?*
She: *Nothing.*
He: *I know there is something bothering you.*
She: *There is nothing wrong. There is nothing bothering me!*
He: *Then why are you looking at me like that?*

She: *I'm not looking at you.*
He: *Yes, you are.*
She: *No, I'm not.*
He: *If you don't tell me what's wrong*
I'm   leaving.
She: *Go ahead and leave.*

Poor communication takes place at home, at work, and in the community. If you care about others, value their friendship, and enjoy their company, it's your responsibility to maintain the relationship by communicating your beliefs and emotions. Do not expect others to read your mind.

Nothing thrives on neglect. You call them. You make the arrangements to get together. You be kind and thoughtful. If they do not reciprocate, you need to make a decision regarding the relationship. Do not fall victim to their mistreatment of you by mistreating them.

You may have different values. You may see the relationship from a different prospective or have different expectations of each other. The only way you will know is by communicating with each other.

You must learn to be assertive, know what you need and express what you want. You must enhance your verbal skills and overcome the emotions that block you from effectively stating your wants, needs, and expectations. You must learn to negotiate and compromise if you want to make and keep meaningful relationships.

The Bounce Back Kid

We are resilient with a natural ability to start over. We recover after loss and rejection. We find happiness after emotional despair. Those who successfully pull themselves up and out of a dark place in their lives, tend to engage in the following behaviors.

Adaptability: They are socially responsive. They are flexible and develop the ability to adapt to change, to "go with the flow." They develop an ability to take things in stride and not over react or become distraught in response to a change in plans or circumstances.

Reflection: They develop a high tolerance for frustration. They come to understand their trigger points, those people and events that set them off emotionally. They try to avoid frustrating situations and attempt to minimize negative outcomes.

Problem Solving: They learn to consider alternatives before making decisions. They seek solutions and view problems as opportunities to be creative thinkers. They become secure enough to avoid "finger pointing" and the need to find fault and blame others.

Self Esteem: They develop "self love" and a "can do" attitude. They have survived experiences that called for self-efficacy, which built a strong sense of self-confidence. They realize they make mistakes and things often don't go as expected. They understand it's not the situation, but how it's handled that validates them as worthy, successful individuals.

Optimism: They developed a positive worldview. They have a good feeling about themselves, others, and life in general. They expect good things to happen and when they do, they recognize them. They are future directed. They expect to succeed and live accordingly.

Affection: They feel comfortable demonstrating affection. They are able to give and accept sincere compliments. They consider physical touch a positive and caring gesture.

Responsibility: They are dependable. They do their best, keep their word, and follow up on promises. They understand others are depending on them. They're validated and find comfort in a sense of belonging.

Social Involvement: They are involved with others and their community. They extend themselves through social activities, service to others, and caring for friends and family. They live beyond meeting their own needs and give to others socially, emotionally, and financially.

Learning Experiences: They seek and enjoy learning new things. Formal education is viewed as an opportunity for growth and enrichment. Casual learning takes place in their day-to-day experiences, which provides them with practical knowledge of the world around them.

To find inner peace, we must come to understand the only certainty is change. We must adapt to survive physically, mentally, and emotionally. We must seek harmony with the world in which we live.

~ The more influential you are, he greater your moral responsibility ~

Chapter 7

Mind Your Own Expectations

A Wedding of Clones

It would be wonderful if you could find the perfect soul mate, that terrific someone to walk hand in hand with you through life. However, this person may or may not ever come along, or they may only be with you for a short time.

A significant other is there to enrich you and compliment you, not to replace you. If this were the case, you could put your efforts into cloning yourself and avoid the enriching diversity and the emotional ups and downs typical within a relationship. It is not the job of your significant other to carry you down the road to happiness and inner peace. It's your job to create and maintain your own happiness within your relationships.

Lose-Lose Situations

We tend to enjoy rearranging the lives of others. Although it doesn't work, it is so much fun! We set up a list of "shall" and "shall nots" and wait for others to violate them. We set expectations based on our needs and values, which can create a lose/lose situation. We set up others for failure because they do not measure up to our standards. When this happens, we feel hurt, resentful, or angry. We also feel entitled to attack them actively or passively. We punish others actively when we yell, criticize, or bully. We punish others passively when we withdraw, isolate, or ignore them.

Sometimes, you begin to question your own worthiness. You may evaluate yourself based on the actions of others, believing you have caused another person to act as they do. You may berate yourself for not being a good son or daughter, a good parent, a good spouse, a good friend, or a good employee. You may wonder if you did the right thing, at the right time, or if you should have done more or less for this individual.

The question is why you feel it is our job to set the standards or make plans for others. Who gave you the right to set expectations for others to fulfill? Even if what you are asking of them is reasonable, they have the right to reject your plan. They have the right to do it their way or not at all. Unless it's a matter of grave harm, it is not your place to interfere with the natural consequences of their behavior.

When you decide to interfere or not to interfere with the decisions of others, you face certain outcomes and consequences. When they ignore your advice, especially if they had a negative outcome, you feel justified in criticizing them. How you handle these situations is one way you learn to get along with, tolerate, or dislike others.

You learn from what they do, what you do, how you interact, and how you respond to these events.

There are situations where the consequence could be so serious you cannot, in good conscience, allow it to occur. If you are dealing with a young child, you cannot allow him to run and play in the street. Obviously, a child of tender years is unable to make life-threatening decisions. As the adult, you have an obligation to protect the child, even from himself. This applies to the teenager who wants to drink and drive. What of the youngster who consistently refuses to feed the family pet? Should the pet be allowed to suffer malnutrition, poor health, and possible death? These consequences are too serious to allow.

There are times when you must make the right decision, even if you face adversity. Some decisions only need to be made once. You do not need to wake up each morning and face the same decision repeatedly. The young child can never be allowed to play in the street. The intoxicated teen can never be allowed to drive a vehicle. The pet must always be fed.

These situations are frustrating because you must resolve a problem you did not create. You feel you will pay the price for someone else's poor decision. Either you allow a negative consequence or yo are forced to try to prevent it.

In either case, you are uncomfortable. To find inner peace, however, you must look inside yourself. You have a moral code, spiritual values, guiding principles, and common sense to help you make sound decisions and do the right thing in these difficult situations.

Fool Me Once, Shame on You. Fool Me Twice, Shame on Me

Finding one's self in these lose-lose situations happens occasionally. Staying in them should never occur a second time.

It is painful to watch those you care about engage in self-destructive behavior. How do you reach the child who drops out of school, the teenager who runs away, or a loved one on the wrong side of the law? How do you prevent someone from slowly killing himself by smoking, drinking, using drugs, or morbid obesity? All you can do is what you can do, not what he must do for himself.

There is a fine line between offering help and creating a dependency. Help is giving assistance for a limited time, within well-defined conditions and circumstances. There is a clear and mutual understanding of the obligations and responsibilities of those involved.

Dependency is help with strings attached—in both directions. The "giver" may have expectations of gratitude and control. The "receiver" may have an attitude of entitlement and personal benefit.

Help is freely given in a time of need. It may involve time or money for a specific purpose, within a given period.

An example would be a coworker whose car breaks down and needs a ride to and from work. You offer to drive him for one week while his car is repaired. He agrees to pay you a given amount of money each day for gas expense. The expectation is that his car will be repaired by the end of the week. You are no longer going to provide transportation and he will no longer pay for gas.

If his car is still not ready, you both have to renegotiate the "help" you are providing. If you don't do this, a dependency relationship begins to develop. You resent his demands on your time and feel he is taking advantage of you, yet you feel obligated to continue "helping." He is in a comfortable routine, has solved his transportation problem, and expects your help to continue. He doesn't understand why you are upset; after all, you offered to help him, he pays for the gas, and all has worked out well. The "dependency dance" is in full swing and it continues. He demands and you deliver.

A common situation of helping versus dependency is alcoholism. If you have a loved one who refuses to give up drinking despite the damage it's doing, you cannot do it for him. He denies it's a problem (he can stop anytime), blames you (his family, the kids, his boss), for his drinking and offers proof that using drugs is much worse than using alcohol (his drinking isn't really that bad.)

His drinking has wasted money and diminished his health. It has caused him to lose jobs and income. It has caused embarrassment and humiliation. It has created social isolation from friends and family. Finally, his drinking has caused others to scorn you for tolerating it.

Still, you try to change him. It cannot be done. Your only decision is if, and for how long, you are willing to live with a person who abuses alcohol. You are not in charge of him. You are in charge of you. How is the "dance of codependency" meeting your needs?

If you come away from a person or situation feeling used or manipulated, it's a flashing red light to stop and think about what is really happening. If this has become a pattern in your life, it's time to look inside yourself. It's easy to point the finger at others and blame them for creating havoc and unease in your life. The real question is why you allow it. Do not let yourself become caught up in other people's drama.

I Am, I Can, and I Will

You need to understand and be willing and able to state your needs and feelings. You must assertively state your position in the matter at hand. Will you be criticized? Possibly. Will you be acting in your best interest and that of others? Yes.

This is what allows you to live comfortably with difficult decisions even if others cannot. Being decisive and assertive will avoid frustration. You don't have to be aggravated by others. You don't have to set yourself up for disappointment. You don't have to offend others or defend yourself.

You need to do what you think is right and make a clear and deliberate decision without pointing the finger at someone else. You don't need to offer an apology or have a list of reasons for your decision.

The Undecided

When we do not make a decision, that is a decision. If you decide to put things off, wait things out, or see how others handle things, you have decided to be passive. You have become reactive instead of proactive. Your non-decision is a decision.

Changes in others or your environment often cause you to pull back and avoid the challenges that come with having to adapt. You become passive and prefer not to make any decision when dealing with new situations.

This often happens when those around you make major life changes such as separation, a divorce, a career shift, or their physical appearance. You have become used to them the way they are, imperfect as that may be. You find comfort in the familiar. Now they have crept into your comfort zone with their changes and we don't like it. It upsets the status-quo.

Change can be threatening to relationships. You must learn to accept this "new" person in your life and respond differently toward him. He was never like this before, why has he changed? How am I supposed to deal with this? I'm upset and it's all his fault! His changes have provided an opportunity for you to criticize him and feel justified in doing so.

Life Enriching Principles

We all have an inner strength that helps minimize our anxiety and calm our fears in the face of change. You can develop behaviors and practice them each day to create personal success and find inner peace.

- Have an open mind. Seek new learning experiences, consider possibilities, and be open to new ideas.

- Never seek to be hurt or offended.

- Never say, "I can't."

- Always put forth your best effort. You get back from the world what you put into it.

- Develop a skill, talent, or expertise and share it with others. You can't give away what you don't have.

- Rid yourself of blame. Take ownership of your life situation and choices. Relieve others of responsibility for your decisions.

- Don't try to justify your resentments. Resentment will destroy you.

- Follow your dreams. Do not die with your potential unused.

- Engage the spiritual part of your inner being. Embrace silence, commune with nature, meditate. Make the mind-body connection.

- Plan each day to make a better new and improved you.

- Unburden yourself from past hurts, accept them, and then let them go. Let go to move on.

- Don't allow your past to carry misery into your future.

- Admit you've made mistakes, were wrong, or made poor choices. Make amends. Commit to change and keep going.

- Don't try to solve a problem with the same mind that created it.

- Have the wisdom to avoid negative thoughts, actions, and people. Negativity weakens us physically, mentally, and spiritually.

- Treat yourself as if you are already where you want to be.

~ Do Unto Others as You Would Have Them Do Unto You ~

Chapter 8

Follow Your Dreams

Think Big, Move Fast

People often fail to pursue their passion because they think it will take too long and believe they have no chance of reaching their goal.

For example, they want to go to college, but it would take them ten years to graduate. *How old will you be in ten years?* If you go to college or you don't go to college, in ten years you will still be ten years older. Since we cannot escape aging, why not begin college now, even if it takes ten years or twenty years to complete your degree? This is true of music lessons, learning to play chess, enjoying photography, or writing your memoir.

We don't have to become an Olympiad to take swimming lessons; we just need to follow our dreams.

Life by Default

Many people resign themselves to a marginal life style. They tolerate less than they deserve. They do this to avoid the risks involved in seeking success. They may find it easier to please others, avoid conflict, or embrace failure than strive for what they really want. They live a minimal existence, unhappy in the present with no hope for the future. They have learned to live with and enjoy their misery.

Why are you settling for less than you want? You have given up on yourself and surrendered to *existing* rather than *living*. Perhaps it's fear—of the unknown, of failure, of trying, of not succeeding. How terrible you might feel to have run the race and lost. Oh, how much worse never to have experienced the thrill of the race, regardless of the outcome. Remember, only one person can win, come in first, or graduate at the top of the class. Does that mean other competitors don't matter? They are not important? How can someone win a race if no one else runs in the race? Without the rest of us, there would be no winner.

Do not settle for life. Do not tolerate life. Do not struggle with life. Face life head on and make it the way you want it to be.

Imagine and Believe

To achieve greatness, to experience success, to find satisfaction, you must first know what you are seeking. It's the difference between fishing and hunting. Fishing, you throw out the net and see what you catch. Hunting, you know what you are looking for and set out deliberately to find it. You do not allow distractions. You overcome barriers. You stay on the trail.

How do you judge success?

What do you need to define yourself as successful? Life can generally be divided into several major areas:

- Physical
- Mental
- Emotional
- Spiritual
- Financial
- Vocational
- Social

The best course is to have balance in all areas of your life, to enjoy success in each of them. Typically, one or the other of these areas spike due to situational demands at various points in your life.

Our physical health is a prime example of a life area that moves into first place at certain times. Without good health, success can be difficult to achieve in one or more of the other areas in life. If you are sickly or disabled it will affect your finances and may cause you to doubt your spiritual beliefs. Illness, especially chronic illness, may cause depression or anxiety. It may limit your relationships and social involvement.

Many quality of life issues are based on good health. We tend to take our health for granted, until we don't have it. We often jeopardize our health with negative habits or excesses. Smoking is a known killer, yet we continue to do it. Food is a good thing, unless we are severely underweight or overweight. Consuming alcoholic beverages can be enjoyable, social, and in some instances, beneficial, but when overdone can be toxic. Prescribed medications can save our life, but taken in excess can end it. Endangering behaviors and a high-risk life style are a threat to good health, yet every day someone is speeding, running a red light, or not using safety equipment.

You may think more is better. More things. More money. More vacations. More friends. Sometimes more is just excessive. Too much of anything can become emotionally overwhelming, physically exhausting, and financially draining.

Excess may manifest itself in acquiring material things or constantly changing from one activity, job, or relationship to the next. The buzz from constant change can be exhausting and keep you from reaching your goals in any of your life areas.

It is up to you to set your goals, expect to achieve them, and avoid barriers to your success.

Who Shot Me in the Foot?

Sometimes we sabotage ourselves. We set up a cycle of failure. There are those who feel their measure of success is reflected in their life style —a big house, an expensive car, or fine clothing. There is nothing wrong with any of these things.

A problem develops when you have to work night and day to afford this life style. There is something wrong, not with the material things, but with your drive to have them as a measure of your worthiness. This forces you to overwork and miss the other important aspects of your life such as health, relationships, and inner peace. The more things you acquire, the longer hours you work to purchase them, the less time you have for pleasurable activities, the fewer interactions with those you love and those who care about you. You also feel you have to work longer or harder to maintain your material goods. You have set up a cycle where you are so busy chopping wood, you have no time to sharpen the axe.

Ready, Aim, Fire

Success is fueled by motivation. Wishing and hoping will not get you where you say you want to be. You must set a goal, make a plan, and take action.

The tasks may seem overwhelming—time is short, resources are limited, or support is not available. Although this may be true, recall that childhood joke:

> *How do you eat an elephant?*
> *One bite at a time.*
> *(To eat a big elephant,*
> *take small bites and eat slowly.)*

Attitude and persistence are the keys to achievement. You must be proactive not reactive in life. You must take action, not sit and watch your life move on without you. You must be in the driver's seat, not in the passenger seat. As the driver, you are faced with decisions, perhaps with disasters, but you are in control of the vehicle. If you are in the passenger seat, you are just along for the ride. Have a strong belief in yourself to deal with obstacles and achieve your goal. Remember your dreams? Where are they now?

Who's In Charge Here?

Control is important. The trick is to control what you can and keep your eye on the rest. Decide what is within your control and understand other things are going to happen. Those with a religious orientation express this as, "Let go and let God."

Here is an example of controlling what you can and letting all else take care of itself. You may have a cranky relative. You dread his phone calls, with all his negative complaints—his family, the government, and the weather. He's the kind of guy who wishes the whole world had a bum knee, so everyone could suffer as he does.

What is within your control? Can you change this curmudgeon to *Mr. Happy Face*? No. Can you change his negative worldview? No. Can you keep him from sharing his strongly held opinions? No.

Here are things you can do to take charge.

- Decide to get him out of your life forever and refuse to answer his calls.

- Tell him never to call you again.

- Insult him, so he refuses to call you again.

- Tell him to stop all the negative comments.

- Tell him to call when he's in a better mood.

- Call him when it is convenient for you and end the call when it becomes unpleasant.

- Call him when you are mentally and emotionally able to handle his tirades.

- Excuse yourself from the phone and offer to call him back later.

- Set a time limit at the outset of his phone call, based on your endurance level.

Granted, nothing has changed with this individual. He is still his same old cranky self. What has changed is how you deal with him. You have changed. He is as crabby as ever. You are being proactive. You are no longer being reactive to his behavior. You are not allowing yourself to suffer at the hands of someone else, and then feel hurt and resentful. You are accepting this person on your terms, under your conditions, and are able to end the relationship or maintain it without feeling used, annoyed, or resentful.

Why Give Up Before It's Over?

Life is never a direct route. It is full of obstacles. This is no reason to stop and give up. Life has detours. A barricade is not a final point, it is a turning point. Your task is to work around those things which stand between you and your goal.

If you were driving on a vacation and had to make a detour, would you turn around and drive back home? You may be upset by the delay, but you'd find another way to get where you were going. After all, you had a plan, put gas in the car, took time off from work, prepaid for accommodations, and called ahead to friends and relatives. Would you throw all of this away because you couldn't go the direct route you had planned? Unlikely.

Likewise, on the road through life, you set goals and make plans. Sometimes it's smooth sailing, sometimes it's rough waters. You must continue your forward movement, confront each set back, assess the alternatives, and make a new plan. Most importantly, you must keep moving.

Is It Really the End of the World?

No matter how many mistakes you make, they are usually momentary and not life altering events. If you fall off the track toward your goal, it means you must recover and keep on going.

If you want to lose 50 pounds and you hit the chips, dip, and dessert during the holidays, it doesn't mean obesity is your final destination. It means tomorrow is a new day to start again to monitor what you eat and drink. If you make poor financial decisions, it doesn't mean you must live in poverty forever. It means you need to get a grip on your income and expenses. You need to make financial repairs and create a plan to avoid these problems in the future. If you are fired, it doesn't mean you will always be unemployed. You must consider what went wrong, learn from it, and apply for another job.

There are of course, some mistakes and poor decisions, which do have life long ramifications. In the moment, it may be disastrous, but a crisis does not last forever. You can adapt. You can change. You can accept responsibility, gain insight into what went wrong, and decide to do the best you can to make things better. You must once again, set a goal, make a new plan, and take action.

Remember, we all do the best we can with what we have at that moment in time. A quality life starts, encounters set backs, and keeps going. If you give up, your final resting place will be engraved with this sad epitaph: *Potential Intact*.

Success and Happiness

Make a list of things that would make you happy. Check off the items you have achieved so far. Remaining arc thc things you feel would make you happy, but do not yet have. Now determine the areas where your needs are not being met.

- Interpersonal/family relationships
- Physical health and well being
- Mental health and emotional balance
- Financial security
- Career/vocational/job satisfaction
- Professional/intellectual/educational growth
- Friends/socialization
- Community involvement/recreation
- Spiritual/religious
- Acceptance/belonging

Persistence is the Key to Success

How do you get the things you think will make you happy? Practice, practice, practice. The more you do something, the better you get and the more likely you are to succeed.

The story is told that Babe Ruth, the baseball great, swung at every pitch, which meant many strikeouts. Yet, what do you remember about *The*

Babe? You remember him as the greatest hitter of all time.

To attain this level of persistence, you must have a realistic view of where you are in life, how you got there, and where you want to be. You must accept responsibility for making the choices which brought you to where you are today. Point the finger toward yourself not at others.

There are many stumbling blocks on the road of life, some very legitimate. You may have had a harsh childhood, medical problems, family obligations, or lived with constant criticism. These events can stop you where you are, set you back, or get you side tracked. You can hide behind any of them and no one would find fault with you for doing so.

However, the successful person goes on in spite of these events. He views an obstacle as a temporary detour toward his goals. When he is able, he goes full steam ahead. When forced to stop, or slow down, he keeps his destination in mind. He never gives up his dream.

If you are unhappy, you must ask yourself these two questions:

1. What do you need to do to make positive changes in your life?

2. Are you willing to work hard and take the risks to do those things?

Do not get lost thinking about what others can do, should do, or didn't do. Perhaps you don't want to do something, you don't see a need to do it, or you are unwilling to do it, but rarely is it true that you "can't" do it. Listen to yourself. What do you say is holding you back? *I don't have the time. I don't have the money. I don't have the energy. I don't have the skill.* Which roadblock has your name on it?

I Want vs I Need

You can do anything if you want to; it is a matter of motivation. How much do you really want to reach your goals? What are you willing to do to reach them? Often it is a trade off of time, money, or convenience. You may have to give up short term pleasures to have long-term satisfaction.

Sometimes we confuse what we want with what we need. It is important to put things in perspective. First, determine what you need and then decide what you want. If you are unrealistic in setting your goals, you will become frustrated, and give up hope.

Let's use money as an example. You may need financial security. You may want to accumulate wealth.

If you need financial security, you have to have money. This alone is not enough. You must have a constant source of income, in predictable amounts, in a specific time frame. You need to create a savings plan for emergencies and a retirement plan for future needs. You must learn how to budget your income and monitor your expenses. This would give you the security of knowing you can provide for yourself and those who depend on you. You would have a certain life style and make decisions based on your income and expenses. Doing these things would meet your need for financial security.

If you want to accumulate wealth, you not only must have money, you must use it wisely. You must educate yourself and seek counsel with others who have achieved financial wealth. This includes making a plan for spending, saving, and investing. If you don't make a plan or don't follow it, you may meet your *need* for financial security, but it's unlikely you will satisfy your *want* to accumulate wealth.

Whether you follow your dreams or not, life will go on. Start now. You can do it.

~ *Do a Kind Deed Each Day* ~

Chapter 9

Keep Your Happiness Beans in Your Own Basket

Why Are You Making Me Unhappy?

You should not expect others to make or keep you on the road to happiness. That is your job. It's unfair to put your "happiness beans" in someone else's basket. Making you happy becomes a tiresome burden and leads to conflict within relationships.

You may expect others to make you happy, or to meet your emotional needs. You create an agenda for how they should go about doing this. If they don't fulfill your fantasy, you arbitrarily decide they don't care about you.

You develop a need to collect evidence to prove this person is or is not making you happy. For example, you may decide if he really loves me he would:

- Kiss me each time we meet
- Say "Love you" when we end a phone conversation
- Hold my hand in public
- Remember my birthday
- Be willing to spend time with my family/friends
- Go to the movie I want to see
- Buy me gifts
- Let me handle the money
- Notice how I look and offer me compliments

You have set up an ambush, which will tare apart your relationship. What happens if he doesn't meet the criteria you have established? You are unhappy and it's all his fault. This only happens because you turn your happiness over to someone else.

Don't saddle others with making you happy. Take charge and make your own happiness. Don't try to sneak your happiness beans into someone else's basket. Your happiness is your responsibility.

If you find yourself saying these things or making similar comments, you are trying to get someone else to make you happy.

- *If he would just love me more*
- *If she would appreciate all I do for her*
- *If she would try to get along with my friends*
- *If he would just show me that he cares*

Somewhere along the way, you decided your happiness was dependent on what someone else says or does. You have put yourself in a position where they will act and you will react. You have allowed yourself to become a passive observer in your life instead of an active participant.

This works well because being unhappy is now someone else's fault. This may work great for you. After all, if you're miserable it's not your fault, it must be the fault of the person holding your happiness beans. You can hide behind the inability of someone else to keep things going smoothly in your life. They are certainly guilty of creating your misery. Shame on those mean, ungrateful people for not doing a better job with your happiness.

You, the Super Star

In truth, your happiness is dependent on the life you make for yourself. This is reflected in your accomplishments, your feelings of worthiness, and the satisfaction you feel with your place in life. You are in charge of your life and your happiness.

How do we create our own happiness? First, recognize your strengths and celebrate your successes. You have done many things well during the course of life. Realistically, there are things you have done to the best of your ability that resulted in personal satisfaction and earned recognition from others. Feel proud of your accomplishments.

Of course, you can take pride in things you do that go unnoticed by others. Sometimes this brings even greater inner satisfaction. You may have completed something that was difficult or took a long time. You may have donated time, goods, or services to others, who are unaware you were their benefactor. These too can create a feeling of satisfaction and accomplishment.

Pleasure can be found in work and in leisure activities, as well as relationships. As a child, you may have won the spelling bee, presented the best book report, or did the most wheelies on your bicycle. You may have graduated in the top third of your class, aced a job interview, or been the youngest person to earn a promotion in your company or attain a military rank. Perhaps you never missed a car payment, were the first in your family to go to college, or started over with only a dollar in your pocket. Maybe you overcame illness, poverty, or negative influences to become a law abiding, tax paying, good citizen. You may have worked extra hours or taken a second job to pay for a family member's medical care or college education. There are many things you have done which brought a feeling of satisfaction and happiness into your life and validated your success.

You have loved and been loved. You have earned the respect of others. You have built relationships based on integrity, hard work, and dependability. You have understood, comforted, and supported those who needed you in their time of sorrow.

Yes, you are a good person and others know all about the goodness in you, because they have experienced it. Perhaps it was a family member, a friend, a coworker, a stranger, but you were kind and thoughtful and they loved you for it. Not everyone may be aware of the things you have done, but you know and should feel proud of and satisfied with yourself. You need to reclaim those moments and events. You need to create more of them.

In your busy life, how do you make your own happiness? You find a need and fill it. You extend yourself beyond what is necessary or expected, and go one step further than what is required.

Our Daily News

There is a wonderful thing about tomorrow. It is a new day. It is 24 hours. It is 1,440 minutes. Each day you have an opportunity to start over. You can make each new day whatever we want it to be.

Take control of your own happiness by making time for yourself. You are worthy of self-care. Are you worthy enough to invest just one-half of one of those 24 hours in yourself? Yes. Are you entitled to 30 minutes of the next 24 hours just for you? Yes.

Are you entitled to 30 minutes of happiness? Absolutely! What could you do to bring joy into your life during those 30 minutes?

Be kind to yourself; don't pick up where the bullies left off. Listen to your inner monologue. Don't repeat the negative things you grew up with or mean comments you overheard from others. Are you really a dopey kid, a lazy bum, a mean son-of-a-gun? Have you allowed others to convenience you that you are worthless or miserable?

You may feel you are undeserving of joy because someone else thinks you are unworthy—and you have now convinced yourself it is true. You now tell yourself you will never amount to anything. You find fault and review all those mistakes along life's way—starting with falling off your bike in second grade.

Do bad things happen? Of course. Is life unfair? Sometimes. There comes a time to move on and leave it behind. If you stay living with hurt, resentment, and anger, lost in the unfairness of it all, you have given your happiness beans to someone else.

Some say the only thing between a rut and a grave is how long we stand there digging. It is time to put down that shovel and move on.

Woe is Me!

What could be worse or more unfair for an actor than full paralysis from a simple fall off a horse? What a terrible blow for a musician who loses his hearing. How could a young girl, having mastered the sea on her surfboard, ever deal with her arm being ripped off by a shark?

These are true events. It is also true these individuals persevered and created success and happiness in new and unique ways. Each could have shut down, withdrawn from life on all levels, and no one would have blamed them. We would understand and offer sympathy. Life had dealt them a severe blow. How would it have helped any of these individuals to give up? What would they have accomplished to abandon all hope and cut themselves off from the world?

Are some of us victimized by our environment or an accident of birth? Absolutely. Life was not going well for a black, female, born into poverty, raised in the South in the 1950s, the victim of abuse and neglect. By her own admission, she grew into a wild, unruly teenager. Could anyone blame her? Wasn't this a predictable outcome given her circumstances? Yes it was, but she overcame these obstacles and became successful and wealthy. She graduated from high school, went to college, and became known worldwide. She developed into one of the most famous, respected, and powerful women in the entertainment industry—Oprah Winfrey.

Do not become confused thinking life is good or bad by comparison with others. If I have no socks, my feet are cold and sore. There are of course those who have no shoes, and those who have no feet. Their situation is much worse than mine is, so I shouldn't complain, by comparison I should feel happy. This may be true, but still I have no socks. I still have my problems to deal with, and I still have my decisions to make about my bare feet. It is not enough to feel happy because someone else is sadder than I am, so by comparison, I feel better. This is not true happiness.

Happiness is not the absence of feeling sad. Happiness is a positive worldview, a personal attitude of feeling good within one's self, and a belief in self-efficacy in dealing with whatever life presents. Happiness is a strong positive belief that I am a lovable, worthy, and capable person deserving of a satisfying life.

Barriers to Personal Goals

It's important to set goals, make plans, and take action. Your goals may be personal, financial, vocational, spiritual, or social relationships. Set a time frame and develop short-term objectives. You must see where you want to go and take specific steps to get yourself there. Invest time each day in your self-development plan.

You are never too old. It is never too late. Each school year we hear news of a college graduate in their sixties, seventies, or those over eighty completing their degree.

You may be sidelined with life's pressing issues, but you must keep asking yourself, "Am I where I want to be?" If not, work your plan and take action. Look at what you may be doing or not doing which keeps you from having what you want. It is quick and easy to blame others or life circumstances, but you also play a part in holding yourself back from self-fulfillment.

We often experience self-made roadblocks. One way we stonewall our success is with the "It's toos." *It's too soon, ... it's too late, ... it's too difficult, ... it's too far, ... it's too cold, ... it's too long, ... it's too complicated.*

Perhaps life is all of these things. Just because it's challenging, doesn't mean you can't do it. Something which takes a long time to achieve simply means the sooner you start, the sooner you finish.

Your Top Ten List

Take a moment and make a list of the ten most important things in your life. Are you on your *Top Ten List*? How important are you to yourself?

If today were your last day on earth, what would you do with your 24 hours? Look carefully at your *Top Ten List*. Who or what is worth your precious last hours of life? Where would you be? Whom would you be with? Whom would you talk to? What would you do?

It's easy for you to become more concerned with the welfare of others than with yourself. You may have allowed your family, children, friends, or employer to take top priority in your life. You may give more attention to your pet than you give to yourself. You take the dog for shots, grooming, and a check up. Have you had your annual physical, gotten yourself a new hairstyle, or had your teeth cleaned recently?

You may take better care of your possessions than you do of yourself. You clean your house and mow the lawn. You take your car for maintenance. You take your clothing to the cleaners. What have you done for yourself lately? Have you read a good book? Have you taken a peaceful walk under the stars? Have you stopped to smell the roses?

What about you? Don't you count? You must come to see yourself as worthy and important. If you don't see yourself as significant, who will? What is the message you give to others about your worthiness?

This is not being selfish. It does not mean self-love to the exclusion of others. It doesn't mean being so wrapped up in your wants you do not have empathy or extend yourself to those in need. It means accepting responsibility to take care of yourself. You have an obligation to stand on your own, be assertive, and establish your independence. It's a heavy burden to expect others to meet your needs or be responsible for your life, happiness, or success. These tasks are yours alone.

Something Out There is Trying to Find Me

Life is a cycle of emotional ups and downs. When we're in that down cycle, it's not time to condemn life and give up hope. It's a time of reflection and wonder. It's a time to take stock in ourselves and review our many successes and accomplishments.

The up cycle is on its way. What will it be? What good thing is going to happen? Focus on things great and small that would bring joy into your life. It might be a hug, a smile, a job promotion, or an unexpected kindness.

Know that low points as well as high points are a part of the big picture in life. Understand and believe good things are out there waiting to happen. Give serious thought to that unknown thing on its way to cheer you up, brighten your day, or give you joy. Be ready for it. Hold out your arms to embrace it. Expect something good to arrive any moment. Know that it will.

Can we hasten good things to come our way? Yes. Move the focus of your thoughts, emotions, and actions from you and the sadness you feel, to something else. The two best ways to do this are to become physically active and be involved with others.

I Can Take Care of Myself

First, you need to get up and move. This will increase blood circulation, which will bring oxygen to your muscles and your brain. This in turn will help you feel physically refreshed and improve your health. Physical activity is a natural "high."

You will feel alive, invigorated, and energized.

Next, consider what you can do for someone else. Perform a *Random Act of Kindness*. I will share an incident from my own life. After purchasing a lawn chair at the local thrift shop, I was unable to fit it into my car. A gentleman stopped and after many attempts, stated, "It won't fit." I thanked him and he left.

Pondering what to do next, a woman pulled up and asked if she could help. We pushed and pulled and angled the chair in various directions, but could not get it into my car. She called her husband. He and their son arrived with a larger vehicle. They began to unload their fishing gear and made room for my chair. They repacked their things in the back seat. They drove to my house and unloaded the chair and then rearranged their fishing gear.

How to thank people like this? I have no idea, but I did "pay it forward." A few days later when a wheelchair bound woman was trying to balance her packages and maneuver through a heavy double door where I was shopping I stopped to offer assistance. A small act of kindness by me was deeply appreciated by her.

What can you do to help others? You could bring up the neighbor's trashcan, move their newspaper to their doorstep or stop to speak with someone out for a walk. Find a good cause and do your part, even if occasionally. Are you an animal lover—try the shelter. Do you enjoy young children—read at a day care center. Do you love books—read for the blind. Are you a coupon clipper—mail the extras to military bases throughout the world. Do you play music—share your talents at a senior center. Do you enjoy cooking—take a meal to the local firehouse.

There are many things you have done and can do again, to enhance your self-esteem and self worth. You need to feel worthy and share with others to create your own happiness.

~ *All things in moderation* ~

Chapter 10

If You Don't Ask, The Answer is Always "No"

Where is That Crystal Ball?

Often, we assume we know what another person is thinking, going to say, or do and we attempt to behave accordingly. We hold back on applying for a job, because we know we won't be hired. We don't ask for a promotion because we know we won't get it. We don't apply to college because we know we won't be accepted. We don't ask for a date, because we know we'll be rejected. We won't join a group, because we know we won't be liked. Ah—we are so into mind reading!

Sometimes you miss out on things you want because you don't allow others the opportunity to make up their own minds. You do it for them with this type of thought process.

No sense asking for a raise, I know she'll turn me down.

I'm not asking him for help, he won't think it's important.

I'd ask him for directions, but he probably won't know either.

I won't waste my time applying for the scholarship, I'll never get it.

You may look at your life and think others didn't offer you support. In reality, you may have denied them the opportunity because you didn't ask for their help. You never told them what you needed. You never asked them for what you wanted. You based your behavior on how you thought they would respond without giving them a chance to decide for themselves.

Who Stepped on My Toe?

Our attempt at mind reading is one way we sabotage our success. We say we want something, but then do not do what is necessary to make it happen. We don't even make an attempt. We don't try to make it happen. We decide up front we won't get what we want. We answer *no*, before we ask the question!

We don't even give ourselves a 50/50 change. By not asking for what we want, we give ourselves a zero chance of getting it. If we ask, there is a possibility of getting what we want. When we get in the habit of thinking and deciding for others it's not usually in our favor. It's not that we asked and were turned down, we never asked. We turned ourselves down.

We should not presume to decide for others. This is what we do when we do not ask for what we want. We make the decision, not the other person. Do not decide for others. We are not so all knowing and all powerful to think and decide for someone else. We need to allow others to make their own decisions.

Guess and Guess Again

Look closely at what you are doing. All behavior, verbal and nonverbal, is a form of communication. It is often painful or difficult to verbalize your feelings, so you may withdraw from others. You do not directly tell them what you want or need. You force them to try to read your mind. You expect them to know what is going on inside your head without telling them. Then you take your turn trying to read their mind, instead of speaking. You are playing a guessing game and there will be no winner.

We have based our behavior on what we think is true, not necessarily what is true. For example, expecting your partner to be home soon, you may hear the squeal of tires in the driveway, and the slam of the car door. You may think the worst: he is angry, he is hurt, he is annoyed. You quickly run through a list of offenses he could be upset about: dinner isn't ready, the kids left toys in the driveway, the bills are unpaid. Based on these thoughts, you may become irritated and resentful. You greet him with a defensive attitude, and a terse comment. This quickly leads to an argument. You are mind reading. Communication has broken down and the relationship is suffering.

Now, let us replay that scene. Perhaps he is not angry at all. Maybe he is excited and is rushing in to tell you he has won the lottery, gotten a promotion, or met an old friend. Maybe there is reason for celebration.

What happened? Anticipatory anxiety took over. You expected a problem and prepared to deal with it. You acted on what you thought was true, not what was true. We have selective perception. We see and hear those things that fit in with our beliefs and we behave accordingly. This can cause strife in our relationships.

Stress vs Distress

Our thoughts and emotions dictate our behavior and can create a self-fulfilling prophecy. We experience anticipatory anxiety, worrying about something that hasn't happened. This leads us to act in a way which may bring about the thing we fear.

We often experience vague feelings of uneasiness. Anxiety permeates our being and we feel pressured and hurried. We are unable to pinpoint the cause of our worry and gradually it becomes generalized to day-to-day events.

It is similar to having a nightmare. We awaken in a state of fear: heart pounding, eyes wide, sweating, a feeling of panic sweeps over us. Once awake we realize there is no monster chasing us down the mountain. We are safe in bed. However, our bodies have undergone the physiological and emotional changes as if the event had actually occurred.

Anxiety works similarly. It wears you out physically and emotionally, as if the event you worried about had taken place. You must take responsibility for what you think, how you feel, and what you do. You have to understand your needs and organize your thoughts into a logical pattern to communicate clearly. You must be willing to express yourself verbally to convey what you want. It is not the responsibility of others to guess what you need. Use your energy to deal with reality, not anticipatory anxiety.

Yes, Yes, and Yes!

We should have the expectation of a *yes* answer. We should know what we want and consider ourselves worthy of having it. We need to feel confident others will respond to us in a positive manner. Use that self-fulfilling prophecy to your advantage. Think *yes* inside your head. Anticipate a positive response to your request. You are competent and likable. There is no reason to expect to be turned down.

Realistically, you can and may receive *no* for an answer. When you ask and are denied, at least it isn't because you didn't ask. You are not the center of the universe. Not all revolves around you. Most of life happens coincidental to your existence. That *no* answer may have nothing to do with you.

There are many reasons why your request may be met with a negative response. It's not necessarily because of you—how you look, what you said, your lack of initiative, or hard work. It could be due to reasons you are not privy to or conditions beyond your control.

Sometimes, it is wise to take *no* for an answer and move on. The time and energy used to try to figure out why you didn't get what you wanted, or resisting the *no* answer, is taking time away for your ability to move forward. If you had gotten a *yes* answer, you would have stopped right there, perhaps in a good place, but you wouldn't move on to whatever is coming next in your life. This is what a *no* answer does. It pushes us forward and forces us to consider new possibilities.

Look Through My Rose Colored Glasses

Much depends on your worldview. This is the way you perceive and internalize yourself as an individual within your culture and as part of the larger world.

When arising each day, what is your mindset? Is it one of optimism? Do you expect to enjoy the day and experience success? Do you assume positive interactions with others? Do others characterize you as decisive, a go-getter, and a winner?

Do you awaken with feelings of foreboding? Do you have a general unease about what today will bring? Are you pessimistic about your ability to do what needs to be done? Do you accept negativity from others in your life? Do you assume the worst outcome? Do others respond by characterizing you as a complainer, a martyr, or a victim?

There is a short story that illustrates an individual's worldview.

Dear Optimist, Pessimist, and Realist,

While you three were discussing, analyzing, and arguing about the water level in that glass, I drank it.

Sincerely,
The Opportunist

Examine your worldview. Do you create high drama at every opportunity or do you make little of great difficulty?

~ Don't fix what ain't broke ~

Chapter 11

If It Hurts, Stop Doing It

The Good Life

Nothing is worth your physical or mental well-being. Do not allow anything—not a person, a job, or money—to come between you and good health. Most things can be replaced, but not your well-being. The wealthiest people in the world can buy good medical care, but they cannot buy good health.

No matter what is bothering you, it is not worth a stroke, heart attack, or mental breakdown. If you were hospitalized, with breathing and feeding tubes, and an intravenous drip, would you worry about the unfinished work at home, on your desk, or at your shop? Would you be concerned about cleaning the house for the holidays or cooking for visitors? If your life was ebbing away, would you worry about your child's school grades or what the neighbors think? It is vital to keep life events in perspective to maintain good health.

Concerns vs. Complaints

There are times when our complaints are legitimate. If we are truly seeking to remedy a problem, we need to approach the individual in the best position to work with us to resolve the issue.

If your child is having problems in school, there is no need to discuss it in the checkout line with the store clerk. If a co-worker is making life miserable for you, the man at the auto repair shop is not likely to be interested.

This is the difference between complaining and problem solving. If we are truly seeking a solution, we must communicate with the person who has the ability and willingness to listen to us and collaborate to find an appropriate solution.

Some, of course, seem to enjoy the pain. They face the day from the victim position and carry on the pity party. There is a big payoff for complaining about that headache, an unreasonable employer, or a troubled teenager.

Our sad state of life can generate a lot of attention. Others reinforce our outlook and foster our reputation as long-suffering. We have their sympathy. They tend to make fewer demands on us and lower their expectations. After all, how can we be on top of our game, when coping with so many problems? Others limit their demands on us to ease our suffering. We now have fewer responsibilities and we can suffer in peace. What a great payoff!

So Happy to Hear of Your Misery

It's been said that 80% of people don't care how bad we feel and the other 20% are glad. Those in the 20% are miserable and enjoy the misery of others. They tend to be ungrateful. They forget all we have done or given up for them. They only ask, "What have you done for me lately?"

When we encounter these individuals, we feel justified doing even less for them. Sadly, we begin to assess our personal value based on their opinion of us rather than measure our worthiness based our own standards. We need to develop and set our own standards of ethics, morality, and responsibility. This is not based on a comparison with the standards of others.

As described earlier, there are times we interact with others on a triangular path. The Karpman Triangle presents a mode of interaction involving one of three ego positions. Within the Karpman Triangle, we move swiftly from Persecutor, to Victim, to Rescuer. These ego states change rapidly based on the response of those with whom we interact. These changes can generate anger, resentment, and guilt.

Your Personal Board of Directors

Take a few minutes and design the perfect life for yourself from this day forward. What would it be like? Whom would you keep in your life? Whom would you invite into your life? What would you do to fill your day? Where would you go, where would you live, what would you enjoy, how would you dress, what would you eat?

Successful companies have skilled and supportive people on their board of directors. Whom would you appoint to your personal board of directors to help run your life?

Here are four steps to create your perfect life:

1. Make a list of problems you would eliminate from your life. A problem is anything that is causing you physical or emotional pain or negative emotions.

2. Create a list of good things you want in your life. These are things you enjoy, bring you comfort, or bring a smile to your face.

3. Look at your two lists. Identify the things you can actually control and accomplish. Prioritize these things as to the cost and time involved.

4. Set your goals, make a plan, and take action. Start now.

Establish a timeline to make your life the way you want it to be. Consider the things you can do and the things you should stop doing.

The things you can do may include a phone call, connecting with relatives, or losing weight. The things you should stop doing may include smoking, procrastination, or arguing. Start your plan of action immediately. Take charge of those things you can control. Do not short circuit yourself with negativity.

Here is an example. Let's look at your health. Most people want to live a long and healthy life. There are specific things to do and not to do to make this happen. If you want to eliminate illness and have good health, these are just a few of the well-known behaviors that lead in that direction.

Things to Do:
- Drink water daily
- Wash your hands often
- Physical activity 30 minutes per day
- Socialize with positive individuals
- Eat healthy foods, including fiber, fresh fruit, and vegetables

- Use your seatbelt
- Use a hands free calling device in the car
- Have a satisfying job, hobby, or vocation
- Love , care, and give to others
- Sleep eight hours per night
- Join a club, social or community group
- Volunteer for a worthy cause to help others

Things to Stop Doing:
- Smoking or vaping
- Using drugs
- Drinking alcohol to excess
- Staying awake late at night
- Engaging in excessive behaviors
- Live, work, or associate with negative people
- Living beyond your financial means
- Deliberately harming yourself or others
- Chronic complaining

Look at these two lists. If your goal is to live a long and healthy life, these are things to do and not to do. How many of these things are a part of your daily routine? It is not enough to say you want something. You must make a plan and do something every day to move toward your goal. You must take action to put yourself in charge of your health and well-being.

Maximize the Positive
Within the Negative

There are those who have lived a healthy life style, yet sustained an injury, had an accident, or contracted a disease, which presents challenges to their quality of life. Some people have life-long medical conditions, not of their own making. This includes such things as Type 1 Diabetes, Sickle Cell Anemia, and Autism. As medical research improves, symptoms may be relieved and a cure may be found. Disease and illness that have no cure at this time must be managed positively to maximize good health and minimize the negative effects of the medical condition.

For example, those with Type 1 Diabetes, should adhere to their medication regime, avoid certain foods, maintain appropriate weight, have adequate sleep, attend to wounds, have regular vision and dental care, and develop healthy life style habits. Doing these things will improve and maintain their quality of life.

You may not be able to cure your medical condition, but you can manage your symptoms. You can limit the negative impact of an injury, illness, or disease by taking charge of your health care and life style.

The Body Wonderful

There are all sorts of germs lurking inside of your body and in your environment. You come into contact with millions of germs and toxins each day. Why are you not ill all of the time?

You have a wonderful body that is prepared to take care of you throughout your life. In return, you need to take care of your body. Many times, you do not do this. You abuse your skin, bones, muscles and organs. You don't get enough sleep to replenish yourself; you don't eat proper foods for good nutrition and energy. You abuse your organs with cigarette smoke and alcohol. You pollute the air you breathe. Still, your body holds up remarkably well.

When do you succumb to poor health? Illness is the result of a failed immune system. When your ability to fight off disease and illness is overwhelmed, you become sick. Illness forces you to rest, eat property, and stop engaging in those things which cause you harm. Most of the time, this leads to recovery. You may need interventions with medication, treatment, or surgery. Fortunately, you live in an age of medical advances, which improves your life with prevention, treatment, and cure.

Think about and understand what you need to do to have a happy and healthy life. Eliminate those things that cause you pain, illness, and unhappiness. Do more things that bring you pleasure and satisfaction. You will enjoy life and bring a positive light into the lives of others. Remember: pain happens, suffering is optional.

~ Don't put beans in your ears ~

Chapter 12

Don't Become the Kind of Person You Don't Like

You: Live and In Color

One day you're sitting watching television with a group of friends and up pops a video of you being ugly with a family member—yelling, shouting, name calling, hurtful remarks, slamming doors. Not a pretty sight. Oh, the shame of it all! The embarrassment.

Could this be the real me? Did I really act like that? Yes, you did—at least on that occasion. Is this the real you? Hopefully not. Keep this video in mind. If someone made a movie of you in action for all the world to see, would it need to be censored?

Life often drives you to distraction. You feel you have turned into someone you don't like—loud, abrasive, offensive, insensitive, insulting, and hurtful toward others. You may be unhappy and miserable all the time. Please, save yourself from becoming the type of person you can't stand!

Graffiti on Your Wall

What if after you hang up the phone, parts of your conversation were spray painted on the wall behind your desk or in your living room? What if all around you could be privy to your comments? Hmm…scary thought.

There are things you say and things you don't say that, although true, may be harmful to others. Before you speak, ask how what you are about to say is going to make things better. How is this information going to improve things? Will these comments harm someone if he or she heard them or was told about them? More than telling something about another, what would your comments tell about you?

You may feel relieved to get something off your chest, or put out in the open, but it may linger forever in the heart of someone else in a negative way. Before you speak, realize there may be harmful and far-reaching consequences.

Once Upon a Child

Go back to your childhood and look through the eyes of the adult you have become. The key is to find the innocent child you once were. Hold out your arms and embrace that trembling youngster. Tell her it's going to be all right. Assure her you're going to take care of her. The little child inside needs to know you are strong and able to take her to a place and time where she will be safe and loved. Don't let that child down. Now is the time. Here is the place. Take charge of your life and take care of your inner self.

No matter how awful the past, how mistreated you were, that was then, this is now. You're an adult. You made it through the good and the bad of your childhood. Perhaps it was joy and peace; perhaps it was torment and madness. You survived.

Some of your memories may be accurate, in which case, your assessment now is the same as it was then. You may recall things you tolerated as a child which still outrage you as an adult. You might boil over with anger at the injustice of it all. You may come to realize how difficult, how unfair, your childhood really was.

As an adult, you may also be able to put things in perspective and see events more realistically. You begin to understand which part of those experiences you still carry with you. How much of that victimized child is still seeking love, comfort, and acceptance in your adult relationships?

Looking back, you can view events of childhood from a different perspective. As an adult, you can reflect on your childhood years with your knowledge of world events, cultural diversity, social values, and life experiences. You can more accurately evaluate the events of childhood and put them in perspective, both positive and negative. This will validate your feelings and shed light on your experiences and family relationships. You will gain a clearer understanding of the people and events, which shaped your developmental years.

As a child, you survived within an environment over which you had little control. Parents and authority figures made your major life decisions. They determined your spiritual direction or lack of it, the school you attended, and the neighborhood in which you lived. They decided your day-to-day living conditions and the social climate to which you were exposed.

You may have been victimized as a child. As an adult, living life from the victim position is like putting a "kick me" sign on your back. You anticipate others will harm you, reject you or take advantage of you. You may have become bitter, negative, or offensive towards others. You decide to beat them to the punch. "If they aren't gong to like me, at least I'll know why." This gives you some element of control. In essence, you invite others to take advantage of you, then feel justified in your anger, hurt, and resentment when they do.

We do this in many different ways. Ask yourself these questions. Do you take on too much? Do you become frazzled and overwhelmed trying too hard? Are you a perfectionist? Do you procrastinate? Do you run to the rescue? Do you take on responsibility for others? Do you need to be in control at all times?

The Line Up

Suppose you find 100 people and ask them for a report. Listen to what others say about you. If there is a pattern—smart, but sarcastic, organized, but a tyrant, hard working, but unpleasable, you need to take heed. Could they all be wrong? If those you know, live with, or work with were asked for three words to describe you, what would those words be? Is there consensus? Which descriptors would you agree or disagree with?

Fact or Fiction

To ignore the facts does not change the facts. Things are what they are, things were what they were. You cannot go back and change your personal history, but you can come to understand it. Now you can review your past through the eyes of the adult you have become.

You can walk a mile in the shoes of those who raised you, loved you, bullied you, cared for you, or teased you. You can understand where they were in their life at that time and why they treated you as they did. The facts of your life will remain the same. In retrospect, you can understand things as an adult that you were unable to grasp through the eyes and mind of the child you were.

It's Just the Way I Am

Just because you have habitually behaved in a certain pattern, doesn't mean it's etched in stone. *I can't help it. It's just the way I am. I've always been this way and I can't see any reason to change at this stage of the game.*

Hmm... maybe you can't see any reason to change, but you might want to check with others in your life. Change is difficult, especially when you have a reputation to live up to or down to, but adaptation is the key to survival. The more you grow the more opportunities you have to change in all areas of your life. You can think differently, you can experience different emotions, and you can respond in a different manner.

Your Inner Child

There you are, that little boy or girl who wants to be loved, accepted, and treated with kindness. Your inner child is crying out to you for support and comfort. It's time for you, the adult, to go back to that little child and embrace him. Take the hand of that child and offer reassurance. Give that child a hug and tell him your love, protection, and caring will be there forever. Assure that little boy or girl, it will all work out. You will make sure there will always be love, happiness, and success in his or her life. If you, the adult, haven't made that happen, now is the time.

You've encountered difficulties in life. Your job was survival: physical and emotional. Hurt and anger from the past can keep your suffering alive and impact on the quality of your life. It is not a matter of right and wrong. You may be justified feeling angry about how you were treated during your childhood. The question is, *How will holding on to this anger help you have a better life now?*

Some of you had the unfortunate experience of growing up in harsh environments, fraught with poverty, negative role models, or abusive family members. Some of you experienced trauma early in life from the death of a parent, chronic illness, or constant rejection. You had to adapt to survive, and it was painful. These experiences affected you and influenced your thoughts, actions, and worldview.

Unfortunately, you may still be responding as you did when you were a child, as if you were still there. You are in a different place in your life now. You can choose the people you want in your life. You can choose where you will live and your life style. You have alternatives. If you don't like your life the way it is, you have the power to change it.

The Line in the Sand

There is a line you will not cross. Whether it's in a relationship, a job, a friendship, or your finances, there is a place you will not go.

You often tolerate too much, for too long. You tend to hold onto the belief things will change and sometimes they do. Sometimes you do. Sometimes you may move your line back and begin to tolerate more than you should.

When there is a consistent pattern of behavior where you feel violated in some way, it's time to look at yourself. You may be compromising your values and quality of life. You may be angry and resentful toward someone else. You blame them for what they are doing to you, instead of realizing you are allowing them to mistreat you. You cannot keep others from doing what they do, but you do not have to tolerate it.

~ Speak kindly, or speak not at all ~

Chapter 13

Toxic People and Situations

Crossing the Rubicon

There is a time in each of our lives when we reach a crossroads. A time when our decision will result in a point of no return. *Do I walk away or do I stay and try harder?*

Is It Me or Is It You?

You may at some point find yourself in relationship quicksand. It is sucking you down and the more you struggle, the more entangled you become. You come away from each encounter feeling upset, frustrated, and angry. You may feel you are dancing with the devil and can't let go. You feel hurt and drained. You may suffer somatic symptoms with pounding headaches, stomach upsets, or vague aches. You may actually feel mentally, emotionally, or physically endangered by association with this individual. You may be pushed to the point of considering harm to another or to yourself.

When do you know it is time to walk away? How many "second chances" do you allow? At what point do you draw the line? A relationship begins to erode when trust is violated. When you are deceived, by either sins of commission or sins of omission, trust begins to falter. You begin to feel uneasy; you begin to have doubts.

Sometimes there is a major incident, which is so hurtful, so offensive, or so intolerable you have no difficulty making the decision to end the relationship. More often, there are subtle changes over time, which create distrust and doubt that leads to the end of the relationship.

Emotionally you travel on a roller coaster of anger, resentment, humiliation, and hurt. You may feel aggression welling up inside of you. You may feel so out of control you think you are going to explode. You have no tolerance for people or day-to-day events in your life. You just can't handle it anymore.

There is also a passive side to these extreme emotions. You may feel so overwhelmed it is easier not to feel at all. You become emotionally numb. You shut down and drag yourself from day to day feeling hopeless and helpless.

Some part of you wants to end the pain and move on but guilt shows its ugly head and you pressure yourself to hang on and give it one more try. You have become reactive to the life you lead.

How long have you felt this way? Has it been weeks, months, or years? What is going to bring about change? You. Don't look to someone else to change to make your life better. You must accept responsibility and make changes in your life.

At times, you set yourself up to be used by others. You throw yourself on the floor and then complain when you are stepped on. You teach others how to treat you and sometimes allow them to take advantage of you.

Remember, you cannot change someone else. The only thing you can change is your own behavior and how you react to others. The first thing to look at in a toxic relationship is your availability. You may be intimately involved or live with someone who mistreats you. You may work with individuals who are deliberately disrespectful or attempt to undermine your efforts. You may have contact with those who make demands on you, then use, and abuse you. Others may manipulate or intimidate you directly or indirectly through others.

You stay entangled with people like this for one of two reasons: responsibility or guilt. You may feel responsible for causing this person's behavior or their life situation. You may feel guilty if we do not stay, stand by this person, and save him from himself.

Best Predictor of Future Behavior: Past Behavior

We have varying levels of sensitivity to the behavior of those we care about. You want to believe in him, you hope that all is well, but the more you doubt the more you find yourself questioning his intentions. At first, you defend him, make excuses, cover up, and rescue. You tend to minimize his behavior and the effect it has on you and others. You want to believe in him and in yourself, after all you chose to love and care about this person. If it doesn't work out you feel you failed. You are vulnerable to feelings of guilt, shame, and loss.

The first time you are betrayed, by word or deed, you have seen him in action. Rarely does this change. You know what he has done, how he has mistreated you and you don't feel good about it. You cannot base the relationship on what you want or how you wish things would be. You must base the relationship on what is. Do a reality check. Remember, the best predictor of future behavior, is past behavior.

Whose Job is it Anyway?

We are sometimes frustrated and confused about the relationship we have with our adult children. Our sense of responsibility to a young child is different from that of an adult child.

You have an obligation to young children to provide them with the basics of food, clothing, and shelter. Most parents and caregivers go beyond survival needs, and offer love, encouragement, and support. Children need to feel safe and secure within their family. They need acceptance, even when they make a mistake, fail in school, or get into conflict with others.

You, as the adult in their lives, must be able to separate the *doer* from the *deed* and offer trust and emotional support. These situations often present opportunities for learning life's lessons about ourselves and our relationships with others. Even when the youngster reaches the age of majority, typically 18, you still feel an obligation to provide a bridge of support as he or she transitions into young adulthood.

The need for love and acceptance is life long. The issue with the adult child in your life is that fine line between helping and enabling. Offering financial support during a medical crisis is different from routinely paying the rent and utility bills for your adult child. He needs the consequences of his behavior and choices, not you. It is not your obligation to provide a safety net each time your child goes astray or creates a challenge in his life. When they are in trouble and you offer to help, it is likely they will remember you when they are in trouble again.

When dealing with a young child, there is an obligation to provide everything the youngster needs to survive at least until he is 18 years of age. You may feel your young adult is still a child, but legally you have no obligation or authority at this point in his life. You must be cautious not to extend yourself to the point you are intruding into his life. At that point, you are meeting your needs, not his needs. A truly successful parent raises a child who can live independently.

I'm Drowning and I Want Company

Some people in your life hold and play the guilt card to exercise control over you. It only works if you allow it. These people can be so toxic they will go down and take you with them.

It's like someone who deliberately jumps overboard. You try to help and offer suggestions to save his life. You throw him a lifeline, and he pushes it away. You throw him a life preserver but he refuses to grab it. You throw him a raft but he won't climb into it.

What is left to do? You could jump overboard and allow him to hold onto you, pull you down with him, and you could drown together. He has made a foolish and perhaps fatal mistake. This is his choice, but he wants you to save him or die trying. He expects you to feel guilty when you are unable to do so. He seeks control by manipulating your emotions.

It is reasonable to offer everything you can without destroying yourself in the process. When you come to the rescue, you feel good about yourself and sometimes solve the immediate problem. In the end, you rob the person of learning how to handle things on his own and have the satisfaction that comes with it. You create a situation where the person feels indebted to you and this often leads to resentment. The outcome may be you feel he is ungrateful and he feels you are interfering.

It Hurts When You Won't Play the Game Any More

It can be painful to give up the game. Let's say your loved one weighs over 300 pounds. You nag, you complain, you remind. What to do? You limit the food in the house, you only buy healthy foods, but still he puts on the pounds. Tension and conflict is always present between you. He resents your nagging and manipulation of the food supply and you resent his unwillingness to cooperate with your efforts for a healthy life style.

Stop playing the game. You are both adults. You both have working brains. You both understand the basic law of physics: to lose weight, you must burn more calories than you take in. That's it. No mystery.

Do you really think he needs you to tell him he's overweight, his health is at risk, and his appearance is a turn off? This person can look in the mirror, suffer physical symptoms, and endure social stigma. Despite all of these negative outcomes, he still chooses to take in more calories than he burns and so he continues to gain weight.

Is he gaining weight because you bought donuts and ice cream? No. Do you weigh 300 pounds? No. It is because even if you bought broccoli and carrots, if he eats more calories than he uses, he will continue to gain weight.

Unless you have a gun to his head, his life style is his decision. It is not your life; it is not your decision. Do not feel guilty because he makes poor choices. Do not try to solve his problem. Do not wear yourself out trying to fix, save, or change someone else. It cannot be done. Consider your choices and the things you can control to take charge of your own life.

A Snake in the Grass

Sometimes, you may invite toxic people into your life and then make it comfortable for them to stay. You may feel you can't live without this person. Didn't you survive before this person came into your life? You found this person, you can find another person.

There is an old story about a farmer and his wife. As they traveled into town, the farmer spotted a snake in the grass. The snake was nearly frozen and almost dead. The farmer took pity on the snake. He picked it up and put it inside his jacket, hoping the warmth would revive it.

As he continued to drive, the snake started to wriggle and slither out of the farmer's jacket. In an attempt to free itself, the snake hissed and bit the farmer on the leg. Angry, the farmer grabbed the snake and hurled it out the window. He began to rant with indignation about the ingratitude of the snake. His wife remained calm.

Finally, she looked at her husband and quietly asked, "Why are you so angry?" The farmer replied the snake owed him his life and should have been grateful instead of hurting him. Well, said the farmer's wife, "You knew it was a snake when you picked it up."

It is difficult to trust someone who has betrayed you. You must consciously make a choice to trust or not to trust. You become vulnerable when you put your trust in others. Trust involves an element of risk. Trust also pays dividends with the joy and comfort you get from the partnership you have willing formed with each other. Do you dare not trust when it has so much to offer?

First, you must trust yourself. You must have the confidence you will make good choices. If it doesn't work out you must be willing to face the consequences and become a stronger person. It is not essential to make a perfect choice every time. Choice enables us to evaluate our decisions, make changes, learn from our mistakes, and grow. These are the building blocks of self-confidence and self-trust.

Pick Your Own Poison

Toxic people will use you and abuse you. They are hostile, demanding, and ungrateful. You experience anxiety at the thought of speaking to or being with these people. An encounter with one of these individuals leaves you feeling emotionally exhausted. You choose your words carefully. You develop a heightened awareness anticipating some form of negativity from this individual.

To avoid being controlled and feeling trapped in a negative relationship, you develop coping strategies. These include limiting your time, money, support, and emotional energy when involved with this person. It demands an element of assertiveness on your part to set the parameters of the relationship up front. You must set boundaries. The ultimate solution may be that you totally avoid this person.

This may be misconstrued by him as rejection, inconsideration, or ingratitude. He is playing the guilt card. He is using emotional blackmail to control you. You have come to believe it is easier to give in to his demands than to stand up for yourself. He causes you to pay a high price if you don't accede to his demands, so you defer to him to avoid conflict.

A curious result of this situation is finding yourself saying "no" when you want to say "yes." Let's say the neighbors invite you and your partner for a BBQ. You would like to get together with these people and enjoy a cook out. You want to go. You want to say "yes."

You begin to think of the last time you got together with them. You recall other similar events on previous occasions with other friends. You feel uneasy.

Your partner didn't want to go. You talked him into it. He wasn't ready on time. He wasn't dressed appropriately. He was a little too loud or too friendly. He took offense at a remark and pouted. You tried to coax him out of his mood. He responded with a belittling comment. You tried to hide your embarrassment with a smile and a short laugh. He accused you of laughing at him and left with a negative comment about how you mistreat him. You were left to apologize. You felt ashamed and uncomfortable. You left as well.

Now you are faced with another invitation. You want to say "yes," but you decide to say "no." Your relationship with your partner has become so unpleasant, privately and publicly, you will give up something you enjoy to avoid negative fallout.

When You Walk Through a Storm Hold Your Head Up High

It's important to remember, you are not responsible for the behavior of others. People may look at those you are with or related to and want to throw you in the same box, but you are not all the same. You are only responsible for your own thoughts, feelings, and actions. Do not take on responsibility for others. Do not allow others to make you feel responsible for someone else.

You may have to distance yourself from those who do not share your values, morals, or standards. You are allowed to do this and not feel guilty about doing so. Again, assertiveness comes into play. You can state your needs without being confrontational or aggressive.

Here is a typical situation. I'll use the example of a woman who complained she and her husband never went out anywhere together. He agreed this was true. Getting ready, preparing to leave, arriving on time all seemed to present an opportunity for conflict.

He planned his day around the event and prepared to leave work with enough time to avoid feeling rushed. She continued doing things up until the last minute. She would change clothes several times, make a phone call as they tried to leave the house, and bring makeup to put on in the car. She created stress and anxiety for both of them because she made certain decisions during the course of her day that affected their going out that evening.

This set up an unpleasant situation for both of them. He was annoyed she hadn't planned ahead and wasn't ready to leave on time. She was annoyed because he accused her of poor planning and being disorganized. This resulted in an argument, which lead to the fact they rarely enjoyed going out with each other.

We often sabotage our relationships. We set ourselves up for failure. We get lost in our own needs and demand that others meet them. When they do not, we are upset and blame them for making us feel this way.

One-liners for Those Who Think They Need to Know

Sometimes people mean well, but put you on the defensive. They can make you feel you owe them an explanation. In these instances, you need to prepare a one-line response that sends the message that you appreciate their interest, but don't want to discuss this matter with them. Here are some examples:

Divorce:
- Comment: "I just heard you and Fred split. What happened?"
- Response: "We divorced two months ago and we're both moving on. Things are going well."

Child in trouble:
- Comment: "I heard Jimmy was kicked out of school. He's always been a handful."

- Response: "Jimmy's having a hard time. We're working with the school to help him."

Illness:

- Comment: "It's terrible being in the hospital. The costs are out of sight and you have to watch they don't make a mistake."
- Response: "Being sick is no picnic. We believe we have good people helping us."

Mother-In-Law:

- Comment: "I'll be happy to bring the turkey. I know you don't like to cook."
- Response: "Cooking is no bother. Why don't you bring an apple pie?"

When to Cut the String

Some relationships are toxic and we must end them. There may be no other way to deal with certain people in our life. It is difficult to close the door forever. It often brings a feeling of failure. It's important to remember a relationship is not one sided. It takes two to make things work.

When your needs are no longer being met, the essence of the relationship ends. This is especially true, when not only are your needs not being met, but there is also constant negativity in the relationship. You may keep up appearances, but whatever brought you together is gone.

Ask these questions of yourself:
- What are my needs?
- Are they healthy?
- What need is being met by staying in this relationship?
- Do I keep people in my life who meet my unhealthy needs?

We grow emotionally and our needs change over time and so do our relationships. What you liked or were willing to tolerate at 18 is different from what will satisfy your needs at 28, 37, 50 or 72. It is alright to want and need to move on in your life. Give yourself permission to do so without feeling guilty.

It could be you are the guilty party. Perhaps, you have hurt or betrayed another, beyond the point of forgiveness and tolerance. You may have to give up the effort to win over this person, concede you are at fault, and suffer the consequences. You must accept the fact you may never regain the love, respect, and trust of this person. Your dogged pursuit of this individual demanding another chance may become another instance of conflict and emotional injury for one or both of you. It is difficult to let it go, yet this may be the final option.

Warning Signs

These are flashing red lights in any relationship that indicate it is toxic and likely needs to come to an end quickly and in the least hurtful manner.

- *Abuse:* physical, verbal, mental, emotional, or sexual toward you or those you care about, including pets.

- *Destruction:* breaking, damaging, or dismantling items deliberately or by neglect or misuse, especially those items which are important or sentimental to you.

- *Fear:* intimidation, threats, or an overriding feeling of uneasiness or of being harmed.

- *Loneliness:* feeling alone even when with this person; or seeking to be alone without him or her.

- *Dread:* wishing you just didn't have to deal with them or their demands any more.

- *Escape*: wishing they would end the relationship so you don't have to

~ *Love the ones you are with* ~

Thank you for taking the time to read

Beyond the Inkblots:

Confusion to Harmony

If you enjoyed it,

please consider telling your friends

and posting a review on

Amazon.com or other online sites.

Word-of-mouth referrals are

an author's best friend

and much appreciated.

~ **Appendix One** ~

Life's Big Questions

Where am I now and how did I get here?

` What decisions did I make?

` What choices did I have?

` Did I consider alternatives?

` What circumstances lead me to c
   choose one path over another?

` What is my worldview?

` Those dreams I had, where are they
   now?

Is this where I want to be?

` Am I living or just existing?

` Do I start each day with eager
   anticipation?

` Am I satisfied with my life and
   myself?

` Do I find comfort in my daily life and the footprint I will leave behind?

` Am I a positive and proactive force in my life?

` Would others consider me a blessing or a bad example in their lives?

What do I want?

` How do I measure my success?

` Where do I find happiness?

` Do I have good health?

` Do I feel financially secure?

` What is my reputation?

` Am I a positive influence on others?

` Have I found satisfaction in my career or accomplishments?

` Do I find comfort in my relationships?

Where do I go from here?

` Am I happy, peaceful, satisfied?

` What have I accomplished?

` Where have I found success?

` When the end is at hand, did I find
    joy in life?

` What is still waiting to be done?

` What is my unfinished business?

How do I get to be where I want to be?

` Have I set a goal, made a plan, and
    taken action?

` Am I willing to invest the time,
    effort, and resources to be in a
    better place?

` Am I willing to take the risks
    involved?

` Is the poison I know, better than the
poison I don't know?

How soon will I begin to move forward?

` When will I be ready to move on?

` What will cause me to take that first

    step?

` Is my motivation based on what I

    want or what I don't want?

` How confident, how determined,

    how motivated   am I to take

    charge of my life?

~ **Appendix Two** ~

A Special Gift of Small Things
(Given to me by Irene M.)

Band-Aid to heal your hurts

Beads to keep you rolling along on the
right path

Balloon to reach your fullest potential

Button to remind you sometimes it's
best to keep you lips closed

Candle to remind you to share your
light with others

Confetti to celebrate your new life
every day

Cotton Ball to cushion the rough place
in the road

Eraser to remind you that you can
start over with a clean slate

Eyes to help you to see the good in
others

Gum to remind you to stick with it;
persistence is the key to success

Jewel because you are more valuable
than the most precious stone

Life Saver reminder to accept help
when offered

Paper Clip to help you hold it together
in times of stress

Penny "In God We Trust"

Rubber Band to be flexible

Sponge to soak up all the knowledge
you can

Tooth Pick to pick out the good in
every situation

Tissue to wipe away the tears

~ **Appendix Three** ~

Assertive Bill of Rights

You have the right to ~

` Judge your own behavior, thoughts, and emotions

` Take responsibility for your behavior, thoughts, emotions and their consequences

` Offer no reasons or excuses to justify your behavior

` Decide if you are responsible for finding solutions to other people's problems

` Say "no" without feeling guilty

` Be illogical at times when making decisions

` Be responsible for your mistakes

` Change your mind

` Say, "I don't know."

` Say, "I don't understand."

` Say, "I don't care."

~ **Appendix Four** ~

Words of Wisdom

Brush your teeth

Clean up after yourself

Don't run with scissors

Eat your vegetables

Follow the rules

Get over yourself

Happiness when shared, is doubled

Honor your parents

Keep the curtain inside the shower

Keep off the RR tracks

Keep your hands and feet to yourself

Let nothing trouble you,

all things are passing

Let sleeping dogs lie

Look both ways before crossing the street

Lower your voice

Once burned, twice shy

One step at a time

Pay it forward

Respect yourself

Snap out of it

Think positive

Try and try again

Turn off the lights when

you leave the room

Share with others

Sit quietly and listen

Wait your turn

Wash your hands

~ ~ ~

~ **Appendix Five** ~

Simple Truths

Life is a do-it-yourself project

Childhood was then, this is now

I cannot change someone else

I must keep my happiness beans in my
own basket

It is not what I say but what I do that
counts

Wherever I go, there I am

The harder I work, the luckier I get

The road to my dreams is always
under construction

I must set goals, make plans, and take
action

Running from a problem, distances me
from the solution

I must control what I can and

keep my eye on the rest

If I don't ask, the answer is always

"No"

Families are related beyond "due us

part"

True friends do not demand

explanations

*Some people enter my life as a
blessing,
others as a bad example*

~ ~ ~

~ **Appendix Six** ~

Stress Indicators

☐ Do as much as possible in the least time

☐ Impatient with delays or interruptions

☐ Need to win at a game to enjoy yourself

☐ Speed up to beat the red light

☐ Unlikely to ask for help with a problem

☐ Overly critical of the way others do things

☐ Frequently checking the time

☐ Spread yourself too thin in terms of your time

☐ Habit of doing more than one thing

at a time

☐ Often feeling angry or irritable

☐ Low tolerance for mistakes made by others

☐ Little time for hobbies or time by yourself

☐ Tend to talk quickly or hasten conversations

☐ Consider yourself hard driving

☐ Friends/family consider you hard driving

☐ Tend to get involved in multiple projects

☐ Feel deadline pressure

☐ Feel guilty if you relax or do nothing

☐ Take on too many responsibilities

~ **Appendix Seven** ~

Positive Actions

Daily

- Eight hours of sleep
- Thirty minutes of physical activity
- Eat at least one piece of fruit
- Drink at least four glasses of water
- Cut 100 calories to reach your ideal weight
- Learn something new
- Reach out to someone

Weekly

- Speak with a friend
- Engage in a family activity
- Clean, fix, organize, or repair something
- Take thirty minutes to relax and do nothing
- Read

Monthly

- Donate your time, money, or resources
- Reserve one hour to do something you enjoy

Always

- Commune with nature to enrich your spiritual self
- Do all things in moderation
- Practice deep breathing and meditation
- Give and seek forgiveness
- Keep a sense of humor
- Laugh as often as you can
- Expect good things to happen

About the Author

Dr. Valerie Allen, psychologist and author, writes fiction, non-fiction, short stories, and children's books. Her professional articles have been published online and in magazines nationwide.

She is a Licensed School Psychologist, Nationally Board Certified School Psychologist, and a Nationally Certified Case Manager. She is a member of the *Florida Association of School Psychologists* and the *National Association of School Psychologists.*

She has been in private practice for many years working with children and families. She has taught students in elementary school through college and university level in undergraduate and graduate programs.

She supports authors as a member of the *Space Coast Writers' Guild*, the *National League of American Pen Women, Cape Canaveral Branch,* and is a co-founder of *Authors for Authors* and has served on the *Board of Directors for the Creative Arts Foundation of Brevard, FL.*

She lives in warm and sunny Florida where she has learned a lot about many things—especially love—while raising her six children.

~ Books by Valerie Allen ~
Amazon.com/author/valerieallen

Non-fiction
Beyond the Inkblots: Confusion to Harmony
Write, Publish, Sell! 2ⁿᵈ Edition Revised

~ ~ ~

Novels

The Prodigal Son
Amazing Grace
Sins of the Father
Suffer the Little Children

~ ~ ~

Short Story Anthologies

A Gift for Mom
Love Stories for Your Valentine
Short Stories for the Man in Your Life
'Tis Herself: Short Story Collection Volume
One
'Tis Herself: Short Story Collection Volume
Two
'Tis Herself: Short Story Collection Volume

Three

~ ~ ~

Children's Books

The Sun and The Moon
Summer School for Smarties
Bad Hair, Good Hat, New Friends

www.ingramcontent.com/pod-product-compliance
Lightning Source LLC
Chambersburg PA
CBHW060615290526
45793CB00001B/38